TOYS

THROUGH THE AGES

TOYS
THROUGH THE AGES

Dan Foley's Story of Playthings
Filled with
History, Folklore, Romance & Nostalgia

A Book for All Ages

ILLUSTRATED

Line Drawings
CHARLOTTE EDMANDS BOWDEN

Photographs
RICHARD MERRILL and Others

CHILTON BOOKS · *Publishers*
A DIVISION OF CHILTON COMPANY
Philadelphia and New York

For

PETER, SUSAN, SARAH,
TIMOTHY *and* JOAN

In Appreciation

To my family, who lived in no end of confusion while toys and books filled the house.

To Charlotte Edmands Bowden, who made the task of writing this book, and others I have written, a pleasure by providing her talent in sketching.

To Mr. Richard Merrill, whose enthusiasm for and knowledge of old toys made him an ideal photographer.

To The Abby Aldrich Rockefeller Folk Art Collection, Colonial Williamsburg, for permission to use photographs from the collection, and to Mrs. Mary C. Black, Curator, for her cooperation. Also, to Mr. Charles Veysey, President, F. A. O. Schwarz; Mr. George Burke, of Margarette Steiff, Ltd.; and Mr. George French for photographs. To Miss Winnifred Foley for technical assistance.

To Dorothy S. Garfield for typing the manuscript and handling the multitude of detail relating to the preparation of this book. To Mrs. Donald Hunt for general editorial assistance.

To Mrs. Priscilla Sawyer Lord for her tireless efforts in various research problems, for assistance with the Bibliography, and for reading the manuscript.

To Miss Margaret Brine for sharing her knowledge and observations and for collecting information during her travels in various parts of the world; also to Mr. George Burke for background material on Margarette Steiff, and to Mrs. Sally Erath of F. A. O. Schwarz for advice and suggestions. To Mr. Frank L. Ball, dean of old toy collectors in America, for bringing to light many forgotten treasures of toyland.

To Mr. Dean A. Fales, Jr., Director, for permission to photograph toys in the Essex Institute Collections and for making available the resources, files, and library facilities of the Museum. Also, to Miss Huldah M. Smith, to Miss Bessom Harris, to Mrs. Charles A. Potter, and to all of the Staff for their generous efforts in my behalf.

To Mrs. Edward A. Rushford, Miss Colette Rushford, and Mr. Robert H. Cumming for making available the Rushford Collections of antique toys, and for permission to photograph certain of the toys for inclusion in this book. (By special arrangement, this notable toy collection, located in Salem, Massachusetts, is available for loan exhibitions to responsible organizations in various parts of the United States.)

To Mr. Charles H. P. Copeland, Librarian of the Salem Public Library, and to his Staff, for making available the resources of the library, and for their unfailing courtesy at all times.

To the members of the Staff of the Boston Athenaeum, and particularly to Miss Margaret Hackett and to Miss Katharine Van Etten Lyford, for sharing their knowledge and enthusiasm.

To Mr. Ernest S. Dodge, Director of the Peabody Museum, and to Mr. Paul O. Blanchette, Museum Librarian, for their generous cooperation.

To Mrs. Amelia McSwiggin Rawding and Mrs. Frances Dianne Robotti for sharing their research files, and to The Honorable Patrick Murray, Museum of Childhood, Edinburgh, Scotland, for help and inspiration.

To:

Abbot Memorial Library
Abbott Memorial Library
Miss Lilly Abbott
The Honorable William H. Bates
Boston Public Library
Dr. and Mrs. Timothy F. Clifford
Mrs. Harry Cobb
Mrs. Francis S. Dane
Mr. Richard Floyd
Mrs. W. W. K. Freeman
Mr. Donald Hunt
Dr. G. L. Laverty

Mr. John Lee
Mrs. John McElhinney
Mrs. John J. Maciejowski
Mrs. Richard Merrill
New York Public Library
Philadelphia Free Library
Southern Highlands Crafters
Mrs. Willard Tomlinson
Mr. and Mrs. Maurice Weiner
The Wenham Historical Society
Mrs. Frances R. Williams
Mrs. Edward Woll

I am grateful to the following authors, their representatives and publishers, for permission to include the selections indicated:

A. C. McClurg & Co., for *Donkey John Visits the Toymakers,* from *Donkey John of the Toy Valley,* by Margaret Warner Morley.

Harcourt, Brace, for *The Wedding Procession of the Rag Doll and the Broom Handle, and Who Was In It,* from *Rootabaga Stories,* by Carl Sandburg.

Dodd, Mead & Co., for *The Gingerbread Boy,* from *The Storytelling Hour,* by Carolyn Sherwin Bailey.

DANIEL J. FOLEY

Introduction

When I was a boy, the museums in Salem, Massachusetts, were open every Sunday afternoon, and it used to be great fun to pay a visit, first to the Peabody Museum and then, down Essex Street a few doors on the opposite side, to the Essex Institute. In great glass cases, painted white, were the treasures brought home from distant parts of the world by the Salem sea captains. As a child, I never tired of looking at these strange and curious objects. There were toys galore from China, Japan, and that port with the magical name of Zanzibar. Costumes, jewelry, portraits, furniture, silver, china, and no end of paintings and prints, along with scores of other objects, captured my imagination.

My favorite toy, which was not meant to be a toy at all, was a single large, round, carved ivory rosary bead which opened in two halves, showing Heaven and Hell. All the intricate detail of these two worlds became very real because of the encased magnifying glass which enlarged the tiny, tiny figures. This curious object had for my childish eyes a strange fascination, shared by dozens of other boys and girls who visited the museum. It held so much, and said so much, in miniature. I knew nothing of theology, although I had heard about these two other worlds in Sunday School; nonetheless, I was always eager to take another look every time I entered the Peabody Museum.

Frequent visits helped me to become familiar with many other displays, and among them were those "funny old-fashioned toys," as I called them. Yet I thought they were great, and if the cases had not been locked, I might have opened them and taken some out for a few minutes of fun — but all I could do was to look. Childhood associations and memories have a way of "sticking with you," like taffy to your hands on a warm day. I thought that some day I might write about toys.

In this book of playthings, I have attempted to open the door, as it were, to the realm of toyland — not so much to present a detailed chronicle of all the toys of childhood produced in modern times as to delineate in words and pictures the story of some of our best-loved toys. To trace in detail even a small number of the thousands of kinds of toys that have been made — particularly those of the past few hundred years — would be to present a catalog for collectors rather than a book for the typical reader. Then, too, to tell in detail who made them and how they were produced would, in some instances, be almost impossible. The records of many of the early toy craftsmen are scarce, even those of nineteenth-century America. However, there are so many facts about playthings that are little known, or that have been forgotten, that it seems worth while to recall some of them.

Here, then, is a blend of nostalgia, wonder, and nonsense, interwoven with history, legend, and romance, culled from the language of childhood. Research has led me to the maxims of philosophers; to letters, memoirs, essays of reminiscence; to novels, old toy catalogs, and a sizable but little-known collection of books on toys. They have become old friends now, and the shelves that hold them must be expanded to make room for more, for there is no end to the story of toys and the lure that they offer. Toys are not toys unless they are fun, and my reason for writing this book is based on the same premise — to provide for grownups the pleasure that comes with recollection and to give to young folks a peep show of the toys of yesteryear.

DANIEL J. FOLEY

Contents

TOYS
THROUGH THE AGES

"Boy in Plaid," 1840–1850, by an unknown artist. A century ago, boys wore plaid and it was fashionable to pose them for their portraits holding toys such as a whip or a hobbyhorse.

Courtesy, The Abby Aldrich Rockefeller Folk Art Collection

Nostalgia, Wonder, and Nonsense

Hobbyhorses and see-saws, jumping jacks and mechanical toys, merry-go-rounds and music boxes, rag dolls, golliwogs and Teddy bears, steam engines and fire trucks — these and dozens of other toys parade across the pages of this book. Some are of ancient origin, but still popular, while others are as new as the latest developments of the Space Age. They tell the story of civilization in miniature, since practically every major scientific discovery, every important historic event, and every whim of fancy in the world of fashion is chronicled in the realm of toys.

The singing bird invented by Hero of Alexandria a century-and-a-half before the time of Christ was considered no less a marvel then than the latest development in space rockets is in our own time. Curiously enough, this mysterious singing bird, operated with water and created by one of the greatest inventors of the ancient world, became the model for a wide variety of toy whistles which have been a part of childhood ever since. Today, hardly a month passes but some new rocket toy or space-age plaything makes its appearance.

Tin soldiers celebrated the victories of Frederick the Great, and their popularity among boys of all ages was dispersed around the world for a period of nearly two hundred years. On the other hand, important happenings of the day often led toymakers to produce strange and unusual objects. At the time of the French Revolution tiny guillotines appeared in the toy market in Paris. Goethe, noted author of *Faust* and other great works, wrote to his mother asking her to purchase one of these novelties for his young son. The horrified grandmother refused and wrote her son a letter of strong reprimand for attempting to amuse the lad with this cruel instrument of punishment.

Jenny Lind, the Swedish nightingale, became the idol of the doll world following her appearance in America in 1850. The rise of the Tammany Hall politicians in New York was commemorated in a coin bank in the 1870's. Teddy Roosevelt gave his name to the Teddy Bear in the early 1900's, and this lovable stuffed toy has been an international favorite for more than fifty years. Mickey Mouse, of movie fame, also had his vogue. So, too, did Pinocchio, from Italy. And these are but a few examples of the way in which toys have chronicled current events. Realizing the impact of toys on the popular mind, merchants and manufacturers have used them in every conceivable way to advertise their prod-

1

ucts since the beginning days of England's Bartholomew Fair more than eight hundred years ago. Toys of tin, wood, and cardboard, paper dolls and trinkets, and dozens of forgotten novelties were manufactured by the carload, bearing the trade names of the best in soap, soda pop, molasses popcorn, and all the practical items that made life easier, more enjoyable, and really worth living. And the latest toy novelty "given away free with ten cents in coin and two box tops," from this kind of cereal or that brand of tea, still fills the bill as an advertising gimmick. It's sure-fire for sales, and people love it.

In every era since the days of the pyramids, children's playthings have been a vital part of everyday life. Dolls of all descriptions, soldiers of tin and iron, Noah's Arks complete with all the animals, automatons, music boxes, toy banks, tops, rattles, noise makers, pull toys, and innumerable other familiar objects have provided endless hours of fun and stimulated the imagination of young folks. The tools of father's occupation, the everyday objects that mother uses in her housekeeping duties, familiar animals of the farmyard and household pets as well, fashioned in miniature — all have their place in toyland. Playing with toys such as these has always been a visible sign of growing up, so important to the ego of a growing child.

Memories of these childhood toys are recalled often at Christmas, and whenever a new toy or some forgotten treasure attracts attention. Yet, few of us can do more than describe vaguely the hobbyhorse received at the age of five, or the jack-in-the-box, which was equally amusing to Grandpa, or the dainty Dresden doll with her wardrobes of silk and satin. The magic land of childhood, which was filled with delight, vanished with the approach of adolescence; so, too, did the toys. Only a small fragment of the millions of toys made in times past, even during the last century, remains to bestir our nostalgia and to record the heritage of childhood.

In a disarmingly reminiscent way, Odell Shepard bared his heart as he expressed his own nostalgic sentiments about the toys he remembered. In *The Joys of Forgetting,* he wrote: "Our toys were almost idols. There was a glamour upon them such as we do not find in the more splendid possessions of our later years, as though a special light fell on them through some window of our hearts that is now blocked up for ever. We loved them, it seems likely, not for any intrinsic beauty or charm of their own, for often they had none, but rather for a supernal loveliness of which they vaguely reminded our fresh and newcome eyes. But however that may be, we loved them with a devotion such as we shall never feel again for any of the things this various world contains, be they ever so splendid or costly." There is more than a little of the child in all of us, and that spirit often shows itself in a blend of wonder and nonsense. The feeling of nostalgia that comes to us in adult life and takes us back in memory often evokes thoughts such as these.

The word "toy" has a variety of meanings. Some of these are in common use in daily speech, but, for the most part, we think little about the words we use. The notion of a toy as most any object that provides fun, amusement or sport is good enough for most of us. Parents think of a toy primarily as any pretty or practical object that keeps a child amused, absorbed, and out of mischief. Its educational value sometimes occurs as an afterthought. Yet the word has many

2

The lure of the toy seller.

meanings, depending on the age of the person using it, the way in which it is used, and the country of the user's origin. The familiar use of "toy" relates to entertainment — fun and sport in its various forms. Yet, it also connotes caprice — implying a trick, an antic or a joke, and when associated with human folly, as it has been through the ages, a toy means a trifle. This word is also used with reference to a pet, such as a lapdog, and more especially and commonly to a model, a trinket, a gewgaw, or a knick-knack. From the Old English *teon* has come the meaning to draw or to lead, hence the pull toy.

Although some toys are especially suited to certain age groups, it is not always practical to limit a toy in this manner. To do so may take all the joy out of the toy, and thus miss the point of *what fun is for*. Then too, fancy toys do not always satisfy a child's needs. When a real drum is not to be had, a youngster soon finds that an upturned kettle or a pan will serve as well, with a pair of clothespins for drumsticks. A doll can be made with the greatest of ease, and so, too, can dozens of other toys. Fortunately, cost does not enter the picture as far as a child is concerned. For children, the point is all summed up in that cryptic thought, "We love what we love."

Children had played with toys for uncounted generations when that noted German educator Friedrich Wilhelm August Froebel introduced the word "kindergarten" to the language at the beginning of the nineteenth century. Froebel developed the theory that play was a form of education. He looked upon toys as tools which taught children to learn by doing, and he championed sturdy playthings that could stand hard usage. Later, Dr. Maria Montessori presented similar theories in Italy, as did John Dewey in America. Champions of progressive education had rather clearly defined views about this new concept of toys. Psychology and psychiatry entered the realm of toyland, and a new dimension was added to the world of playthings — educational toys.

The importance of toys as teaching aids for youngsters in school and in the home has been emphasized greatly in recent years. At times, it would seem that too much emphasis has been placed on this kind of evaluation. To discerning folk, this often seems a strange approach to the realm of toyland, for playthings have always had unlimited value in teaching children a variety of things. One wonders if a child ever gives the slightest thought to what he is learning when he is playing. Probably not, nor does it matter! Toys speak for themselves, and their value to a child is gauged primarily by how much fun he or she can have with a given toy.

When the twentieth century introduced new and complex notions about toys as we know them, the old ideas about *toys as toys* came to mean something new and different to the adults who bought them, but the children who played with them were not much concerned. Curiously enough, creative research has not always produced toys that children love and cuddle for any great period of time; nor have the thousands of novelties and gimmicks of our great age of mass production been completely satisfying. Somehow, the long-time favorites that had their origin in Germany several centuries ago seem to hold their popularity, and others like them made in Japan and other countries, or even in America, still retain the most enduring kind of appeal. The idea that manufacturers must produce something new each season is important from the point of view of com-

4

merce and the ever-growing toy market, but, all too often, the child's point of view is overlooked. Although the pattern is changing, parents and adult relatives still purchase most of the toys sold. However, children are rapidly becoming aware of the latest fashion in toys because of television, and they express their preferences without the slightest hesitation.

Who first made what and when is a question that rises frequently among toy historians and collectors. When an idea for a toy is developed and an individual plaything is patented, most people think of it as original at the source that claims it, but such is not always the case. Johnnie's whistle and Mary's doll may take a curious individual to many countries in the search for its source. The art of copying and adapting is not new by any means, nor is the notion of swapping and even pirating ideas. Copyrights for the same article have been taken out in several countries, sometimes by the same person using a different name.

Thus, the pursuit of old toys can have all the overtones of a "who done it," and tracing down origins can offer all the appeal of Scotland Yard without any disastrous consequences. There is something about the rediscovery of an old toy, or even a picture of one, that gives us what is known as complete recall of memory. From this kind of recollection we develop a sense of historical perspective which gives a subtle kind of meaning to the things we enjoy. We see these toys as a great panorama, woven or blended to make the tapestry that is the backdrop of life. Then it is that the nostalgic appeal of old toys grows, even though we realize that the realm of Toyland as we knew it in childhood is closed to us forever. Glen MacDonough expressed it sentimentally when he wrote these words for Victor Herbert's *Babes in Toyland:*

> Toyland! Toyland!
> Dear little girl and boyland,
> While you dwell within it,
> You are ever happy then.
> Childhood's joyland,
> Mystical, merry Toyland!
> Once you pass its borders,
> You can ne'er return again.

And yet a new kind of experience unfolds as we pursue the story of toys from the days of the Pharaohs to the present. As we look at them again, they bring into sharp focus things we remember, and many others long forgotten. Toys tell a many-sided story in a most enchanting way.

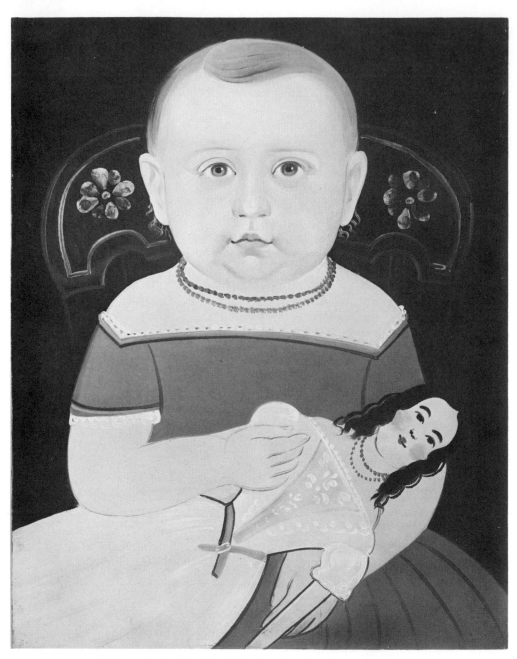

"Baby with Doll," 1840–1850. Attributed to Sturtevant J. Hamblin (Massachusetts).

Courtesy, The Abby Aldrich Rockefeller Folk Art Collection

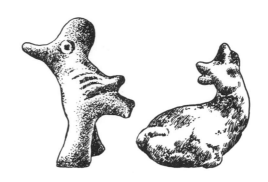

CHAPTER

Playthings of Ancient Times

A clue to the exact dates of two typical examples of early playthings is given us by a strange wedge-shaped inscription, known as cuneiform, found on a temple in the ancient city of Susa in Persia. Carl Gröber, in writing about the toys of antiquity in his *Children's Toys of Bygone Days,* has painted a vivid picture of the laying of the cornerstone for this age-old edifice, which occurred eleven hundred years before the time of Christ. "The onlookers threw into the excavation small objects made of all manner of materials; and among these pious offerings there were found two little animals made of white limestone; a little pig — or could it be a porcupine — and a small lion on a stand with wheels. The little animals could be drawn about by a string which was threaded through a hole in the stand. Little and insignificant as these two objects may be, they are yet of the greatest importance as representing the earliest children's toys which we can definitely date. From ancient Babylon the solitary find of this kind to be known is a fragment of an alabaster doll with movable arms; otherwise, nothing remains which can definitely be labeled a toy. If here or there little clay horsemen or vessels have been found, as in Smyrna, in excavations of the sites of the cities of ancient Israel, these must almost without exception be regarded as funeral offerings, made for that purpose."

Among miniature objects which remain from the pre-Christian era many, when first examined, appear to have been toys. Yet, such is not always the case, as students of early culture have pointed out, using as examples the ornamental rattles which are so attractive in design and coloring as to look like the most appealing of toys. Emanuel Herick, noted Czechoslovakian toy expert, in his book *Folk Toys,* describes and illustrates this collection of clay rattles, decorated much like Easter eggs. They belong to the period between the Bronze and the Iron Age. Some are shaped like poppy heads, onions, and pumpkins, while others are pear-shaped or egg-like in form. There are also birds and animal heads, all suggestive of the influence of natural forms. Actually, these are believed to have been used as ritual burial objects long before they were given to crying babies to quiet them. The reasoning behind this conviction is based on a knowledge of customs and traditions of this remote era.

In the Stone Age, musical instruments made of bone, shaped somewhat like

7

flutes, were in use, and it is believed that such percussion instruments as drums and xylophones were also known at the time. Did children of this period, in attempting to mimic their elders, make similar toy instruments for their own amusement? We can only conjecture that such might have been the case. In any event, scholars tell us that toys, even in early times, were found only in communities where the people had attained a level far removed from that of the savage. Primitive people, whose tribal ways and customs showed no tendency toward advancement in their way of life, were so busy trying to exist that there was little or no time to develop the art of living. Thus, the search for information about the earliest toys known to man brings us face to face with a plethora of details about the very beginnings of civilization, and verifies the old truism that toys reflect in miniature the progress of man.

A dried gourd was probably the first rattle, and may be the oldest known toy, but there are those who would dispute this statement. Actually, there are many toys whose origins are so remote that it would take a group of scholastic philosophers to decide the question. Many folk are inclined to believe that the doll holds first place among antique toys, but dolls were fetishes and idols before they were used to brighten the child's world of make-believe.

Toys which antedate the Christian era include animals made of clay, dolls of various types (including those with movable joints), balls, clappers, sleds, kites, and even playthings on wheels. Such favorites as automatons, hobbyhorses, whistles, toy soldiers and various kinds of edible toys also belong in this category, but they are merely mentioned here, since they are discussed in detail in the chapters that follow. Tops, hoops, marbles, and a dozen other toys have a storied past which has been recorded in paintings, prints, and old woodcuts.

In several countries which border the shores of the Mediterranean, miniature clay figures of horses and riders have been unearthed. Although these are considered to have had some religious significance originally, it is a curious fact that they have become models for a number of our present-day toys.

A considerable group of early toys has been unearthed in Egypt, some of which were found in a remarkable state of preservation, even to the color in which they had been painted originally. This fact has been attributed to the favorable climatic conditions of the country. Wood, being plentiful, has long been a favorite material for toys, but it does not have the lasting qualities of terra cotta, stone, and various metals. Hence, it is easy to understand why not too many wooden toys have survived. Rag dolls and those made of cloth or yarn seldom last more than a few years because of the wear and tear to which they are subjected. Yet, there is an early Coptic yarn doll preserved in a most remarkable state in Vienna which is believed to have been made about the year A.D. 500.

When we think of the hard usage the average toy gets, and how unappealing playthings are when they become shoddy and cannot be restored easily, it is remarkable how many truly old toys have survived. Then too, if we consider the matter of breakage and the custom of putting toys away or discarding them as children grow beyond them, it is all the more surprising that we have so much important tangible evidence of ancient playthings.

Toy animals, some on wheels, indicate that pull toys are older than is generally believed. Many have survived from Egypt, Greece, Italy, and other countries.

8

Among the classic examples are a wooden horse with its rear wheel missing, which can be seen in the British Museum, along with a clay figure of a boy riding a goose. Traceable to India is a terra cotta figure of a man on a unicorn which is dated a century before the time of Christ. From Babylonia has come a gaming board with inlays of shell and lapis lazuli, which is older than the modern world.

In the Leyden Museum in Holland may be seen one of the most remarkable of all the ancient toys that have survived. Although crudely made, it is a jointed figure with movable arms and legs which kneads dough when a string is pulled. It has also been suggested that the toy figure may have been grinding corn. At any rate, here is an ancient example — made nearly two thousand years before the time of Christ — that serves as the model for all the simple movable toys that have been made in the past several thousand years.

What we know as jackstones, also called knucklebones and dibstones, had their roots in many parts of the world where games were enjoyed with them by the children of primitive tribes. Games involving playing cards were also known at an early date in both Europe and Asia.

Not only is the ball linked with antiquity, but with world-wide popularity as a toy, and versatility of use as well. In both ancient and modern times, this commonest of playthings has provided fun for youngsters and grownups and is the object of prime interest in perhaps more kinds of games than any other single toy. It can be kicked or caught, bounced or thrown, rolled or batted. And no toy has probably been the basis for more neighborhood disputes than the lowly ball. It has been fashioned from a number of materials, depending on the country in which it was made and used. In the British Museum there is a ball made of stone that is five thousand years old. Leather balls made from animal skins were filled with bran, husks or human hair, feathers or fig seed. Others have been made from papyrus, plaited rushes, wood, pottery, celluloid, rubber, plastic, and metal. Games played with a ball include stool ball, grap ball, football, baseball, soccer, skittles, cricket, bowling on the green, and dozens of folk games and sports which are enjoyed over most of the world.

Balls found behind the altars in European cathedrals remind us of earlier days when choirboys played ball in church on certain occasions. Anatole France's famous story of Medieval times, recounting the performance of the juggler before a figure of the Virgin Mary, is another example of play with a ball that differs considerably from present-day activity on the back lot. Balls striped blue and gray, of shiny glazed terra cotta made in pre-Christian Egypt, could not be bounced like those made of India rubber produced in the nineteenth century. Yet, place a colored rubber ball beside one of the striped terra cotta type and there is little difference to be noted. Many hundreds of years ago, the bladder from a sheep or a goat provided the first ball that would bounce.

Although the Chinese were flying kites a full thousand years before the time of Christ, and the Greeks and Romans knew them at an early date, they were little known in Europe until the sixteenth century. In China it was believed that the kite had the power to clear the skies of storms and carry evil away. When a kite was first flown in Europe is not known, but it is believed that the earliest ones were brought home by the adventurous Dutch traders. Benjamin Franklin's experiments with electricity were linked with a kite, and as a result he helped to

popularize the kite more than two hundred years ago, when toys were none too plentiful in the Colonies. Wonderful stories about kites and the uses to which they were put in times of war and peace make the subject of kites worth pursuing.

It is generally believed that the sled, the best of toys for winter, is also man's oldest means of conveyance. Necessity is often the mother of invention; when some prehistoric hunter, seeking food in winter, dragged home on a skin the animal he had shot, he made the first sled. A wooden sled runner found in Finland has been dated from 6500 B.C. Skis came into use several thousand years later. However, the first steering sled, the American Flexible Flyer, did not appear until 1889.

In all probability the top originated in Japan, where spinning this popular toy has been developed into a precise science. The children of Persia, China, and India, as well as those in remote corners of the earth, have long shared this favorite pastime with their parents. In some countries it has become a form of professional entertainment. In the Orient there are hundreds of kinds of tops, most of which are completely unknown elsewhere. The Chinese played with one made of ground conch shells, weighted with lead. Other tops are the priest top, so called because it resembles the shaved head of an Oriental clergyman, one for whipping on ice, a pinching top, a catching top, and a fighting top, as well as a humming, or thunder top, and many others. There are kinds that whistle and others with tiny lanterns. The story of tops and the fun which they have provided for the children of Europe and America is fascinating. Tops are not as popular today as they once were.

The toys of the ancients, no less than those of the twentieth century, serve the same purpose — to provide some means of amusement. In every stage of life, man finds some object to fill his need and absorb his interest. Alexander Pope, in his *Essay on Man,* has summed it up crisply:

> Behold the child, by Nature's kindly law
> Pleased with a rattle, tickled with a straw:
> Some livelier plaything gives his youth delight,
> A little louder but as empty quite:
> Scarfs, garters, gold amuse his riper stage,
> And beads and prayer-book are the toys of age.
> Pleased with this bauble still, as that before,
> Till tired he sleeps, and life's poor play is o'er.

CHAPTER 3

The Christ Child and the Hobbyhorse

Although the legends and the lore that surround the Christ Child are the heritage of the whole world, their appeal has always been strongest among plain folk. With each telling, these golden tales have been embellished, enriched and colored by events and trends that were current at the time. This tinsel often seems like so much glitter when compared with the simple unadorned Biblical narrative. Yet, myth and legend are a vital part of folk tradition, inspired by the love of a story. Paintings and drawings expressed the same contemporary feeling. In the fifteenth century, an unknown artist of Dutch or German origin made a drawing of St. Dorothy, accompanied by the Christ Child riding a hobbyhorse. Since children of the period loved this simple toy, the artist thought it appropriate to provide one for the Infant Saviour. This print remains as a warmly human concept of the Holy Child in an era when the folk interpreted everything in which they believed in terms of their own creature comforts.

Actually, St. Dorothy lived in the fourth century, but this fact was in no way inconsistent to the artist who drew the picture, more than a thousand years later. He simply portrayed these two heroic personages in terms of the world he knew and lived in. Yet, Strickland Gibson, noted English folklorist and toy historian, wrote of this picture: "The Infant Christ, who is shown riding cockhorse, is a very happy concept, since the hobbyhorse may well have been one of the toys actually known to the Christ Child."

However, the horse, the friend of man, was modeled as a toy at a much earlier time. Toy horses made of clay, preserved in important museums, can be traced back to the days of the Pharaohs. They were popular in the Orient at an early date, also. Since that time tin, wood, various kinds of metal, cardboard, and plastic have served as the materials to make all types and kinds of horses, big and little.

From Medieval times to the nineteenth century, morris-dancers provided no end of merriment and laughter as they pranced around in wooden frames shaped like horses' bodies. Every touch of realism, from the skillfully shaped horse's head to his shaggy tail, was included in the costume which the dancer wore. Long blankets or strips of cloth concealed his legs, and there was sufficient space within the frame itself to allow for considerable cavorting about and all the "high jinks"

11

and nonsense which his audience would endure. May Day, the Christmas season, and other festive periods throughout the year, from seed time to harvest, afforded opportunity for public appearances. These revels provided sport for all ages, either at the fairs, in the public squares, or at the houses of the wealthy. More than anything else, they provided the comic touch. And the children mimicked them in their own inimitable way as they rode their toy hobbyhorses.

Saint Dorothy and the Christ Child.

A handsome silk wall hanging, woven in the fourteenth century, shows a group of Chinese youngsters riding hobbyhorses with wooden wheels. The carefully designed heads of the horses, complete with mane painted on wood and well-made reins, indicate not only good craftsmanship, but also a highly developed toy. This broom-handle or stick-type horse has remained popular for centuries. Some of the early kinds pictured were rather crudely made, but regardless of the material used or the manner in which it was made, the horse's head mounted on a stick served the purpose for which it was intended. As the Old English nursery rhyme has it,

> I had a little hobbyhorse
> And it was dapple gray.
> Its head was made of pea-straw
> Its tail was made of hay.

They were sold at the summer fairs, everywhere in Europe, and every toy seller carried them in his pack in the old days. Sometimes the "sticks" were long enough for as many as three children to ride astride.

The horse on rockers and the type with wheels attached to all four legs were most welcome improvements in the eyes of young folks, for they made the ride

12

more exciting, even though the fall at times was more disastrous. As tin and iron became popular in toy making in the early part of the nineteenth century, mechanical horses, the horse and wagon, coaches, buggies, fire trucks, and every kind of vehicle a horse was expected to pull were introduced. These added further excitement to everyday play. Today, the rocking horse in all its variations, even when modified to serve as both a toy and a restrainer in which baby is kept confined to his seat by straps and trays, remains with us as a favorite toy.

There are stories galore about dutiful fathers who also enjoyed playing at horses. One concerns a king who lived in Sparta more than four hundred years before the time of Christ, named Aegeilias, who made a hobbyhorse for his children. He was playing with them, probably showing them how to have the most fun with the horse, when a friend called unexpectedly. The chagrined king begged his friend not to divulge this bit of child's play on his part, but somehow the story has come down to us. A similar tale has been told about Socrates, and modern history contains many a colorful yarn concerning great men who enjoyed this favorite form of child play. Playing *pickaback* stems from the same tradition, and imitating the colorful tournaments so popular in the Middle Ages is still good fun.

The Miracle and Mystery plays which were exceedingly popular during the Middle Ages created an image of the Christ Child that was intensely personal. In dramatizing His Birth, the shepherds and the folk were usually portrayed bringing Him gifts. These tokens included bells, a gourd flask, a spoon with which to eat porridge, a tiny shepherd's horn, probably made from a cow's horn, and a nut hook, a handy gadget commonly used by shepherds to pull down branches and gather nuts. To keep Him warm, there were various kinds of garments made of wool and leather, including a cape and a hood. Other items brought by the shepherds to amuse the Christ Child were a bob of cherries, a ball, and a pipe or flute made from a reed. These toys were popular with children at the time, and many of them had been known for so long that their origin was buried in the distant past. In later centuries, when St. Nicholas was somewhat replaced as the bringer of gifts, children were told that it was the Christ Child who decorated their Christmas trees and brought them their gifts, too.

It was St. Francis who brought a new kind of glory to the Christmas crib in 1223 at Greccio in the Umbrian Hills. The traditional reverence for it was not new by any means, but he it was who brought the message of Christ's birth very close to the people of his time, and the image of his simple approach to the Ageless Story has never faded. Thus it was that miniature Christmas cribs eventually came to be the chief objects of interest in homes at Christmas.

The entire family participated in actually making the doll-like figures from wood or clay and arranging them to create a little scene of the Holy Land. Eventually, the Christmas crib came to be associated with the Christmas tree and was often placed near the tree or at the base of it, particularly in German homes. Originally, these Nativity settings had been staged in churches and chapels and in the homes of the wealthy at Christmas. Their introduction into the typical peasant home, together with the Christmas tree, stemmed from the desire of the folk to perpetuate some of the spirit and the warmth of the Birth of Christ, as it was presented in the Miracle and Mystery plays. Performances of

13

these popular plays had been halted because of the many abuses of sacred themes that crept in as they came to be presented in the speech of the day. The comic elements became coarse and vulgar, much to the displeasure of the clergy.

In the sixteenth century, the first Grand Duke of Tuscany owned a mechanical crib in which the heavens opened, as angels flew about and then came down to earth. The figures in the manger scene walked and moved with ease in a natural manner. At Munster, in Germany, a skilled craftsman named Hans Brabender made a clockwork crib in which the Magi bowed to the Christ Child. These were only two extraordinary examples of crib-making before its heydey in the centuries that followed. A letter written by a Bavarian princess to her brother in Munich in 1577 requested figures for her crib setting to keep her fifteen children happy. She stated that, if he wished to send them, they should be strongly made, since they would have to stand hard wear. The vogue for dressed figures was already popular, according to the letter. Crib art became so important that craftsmen and artists became specialists, as they did later in Italy and other countries.

It was in Naples, beginning in the seventeenth century, that the Christmas crib, or *presepio,* as it is called in Italy, developed into a popular art. Workers in the trade were known as *figurari,* and the crib figures which they made were called *pastori.* Along with wooden figures, some were made like puppets, using rags for the body, which were wound on wire. The head, feet, and hands were superbly fashioned in porcelain, and many of these parts were made in the famous factory of Capo di Monte.

Two men of widely different outlook, the Bourbon King Carlo III and a Dominican Friar, Gregorio Maria Rocco, were the leaders of what came to be a most amazing pastime. Unlike many sovereigns, Carlo III had a flair for things mechanical and took great pleasure in making elaborate settings for the Christmas crib which was set up in his castle each year on Christmas Eve. Normally, these matters were attended to by the servants, but not so in this instance. What is even more surprising, the queen shared her husband's enthusiasm and she, together with her ladies-in-waiting, occupied themselves by making the costumes for the various figures. It is said that one of the Magi in King Carlo's *presepio* actually wore a miniature reproduction of his mantle as Grand Master of the Order of St. Gennaro.

Members of the court took up the hobby of their sovereigns, and it was not long before the *presepio* took on social as well as religious significance. As with the decorating of Christmas trees in later centuries, the nobility vied with one another in making these cribs, and soon it became fashionable to visit the homes of those who had built unusual and magnificent *presepi.* They became the talk of the realm.

In Naples the crib became a dream right out of Paradise, sparkling with all the florid color of Neapolitan elegance. Sometimes the entire cycle or several scenes of the Nativity story were depicted. Especially popular were the episodes featuring the shepherds, the Magi and the incident at the inn. In *The Christmas Crib,* Nesta de Robeck wrote:

14

"The scene of the inn gave the *figurari* a chance they certainly made the most of; there could be seen every variety of macaroni and fish, sausages and wines from Ischia or Capri, while a countryman unloads a cart of victuals, a salesman displays his goods, beggars hold out a hand, minstrels play the guitar or hurdy-gurdy, and the guests eat and drink and gamble. It is an *Allegro con brio* from a Neapolitan opera and is continued in the procession

An old German Woodcut.

of the Kings decked out like princes from the Arabian Nights, laden with jeweled gifts, accompanied by slaves, camels, elephants, monkeys, horses, birds, and dogs, and this colorful cavalcade was completed by another of beautiful eastern princesses known as Georgine. The great ladies and gentlemen of Naples were to be found in the Crib alongside every kind of person from every province, cityfolk and countryfolk, all dressed in the right clothes, and in a setting which included every conceivable object known to daily life, each and all represented in perfect miniature models. No wonder that the *presepio* gave work to such a host of people, of all the professions and arts."

With so much interest on the part of royalty in these colorful settings, it was to be expected that the common folk too might become interested. And they did, through the influence of a Dominican friar, Gregorio Maria Rocco. A crusader for moral and civic betterment, he succeeded in establishing the city's first municipal lighting system. At the time, vice and crime constituted a serious problem in Naples. With inspired words and warmhearted deeds, he exhorted the citizens to erect more than four hundred shrines in the darkest corners of the city streets. These shrines were lighted with votive lamps, the

15

oil being supplied by the populace, who filled them when they went to pray. Rocco made his way into the slums of the city, and when sermons and plain talk failed to reach the ears of the evildoers, he was known to chastise them with the persuasion of his staff and his large wooden rosary.

Like St. Francis at an earlier date, Rocco cherished the Nativity story with great reverence and thought that its visual representation in the form of a *presepio* could not fail to have a chastening effect on the most hardened of sinners. Following the tradition set by King Carlo and the noble families of the kingdom, he launched a campaign urging every family in Naples, no matter how poor, to build a *presepio,* and he often helped his parishioners to make them.

In 1787, Goethe, the German playwright and novelist, wrote of the great vogue for these Christmas cribs in his *Italian Travel.* "The representation has ascended in merry Naples to the flat house-roofs; there a slight scaffold in hut-manner is erected, decorated with evergreen trees and shrubs. The Madonna, the Child, and all surrounding persons are dressed up in the most precious manner, and the proprietors spend large sums for the vestments. The whole is incomparably glorified by the background, that is the Vesuvius, and its surroundings."

Turning to Germany again, we find that Munich has probably the greatest collection of Christmas cribs in the world, due to the interest of a Munich banker, Max Schmederer. It was during a long winter illness that he decided to build a crib. Because he found so much pleasure in this avocation, he began to collect cribs. He assembled more and more of them, until they completely filled a whole storey of his large Munich house. Moreover, he had a flair for arranging the figures, which he acquired in his travels, in the most artistic way. To those who did not understand this unusual hobby of an old bachelor, he came to be known as the "crib-fool." In 1892, Max Schmederer donated his whole collection of about eight thousand figures to the Bavarian National Museum in Munich.

As the years passed, come Christmas, the toy markets in Italy and France, Spain and Germany and other Catholic countries were filled with toy figures of clay and plaster, painted in bright colors, representing the Christ Child in His cradle, Mary, Joseph, and all the other Nativity personages. Tiny statues of the Wise Men, Melchior, Caspar, and Balthazar, attired in their gorgeous robes, each bearing a gift, were sold by the thousands. Miniature stables with oxen and donkeys, angels, toy stars, shepherds with their sheep, individual sheep and lambs, dogs, together with peasant figures galore, and those of the Pope and various clerical personages, were sold along the streets by peddlers and at the Christmas fairs. In Italy they were known as *Santi belli,* beautiful saints, and in Provence, in the south of France, they were called *santons,* little saints. Spain and Portugal also produced them in quantity. Children were eager to have as many as they could obtain, for these toys made the long Christmas season all the more enjoyable. It started with fairs in early December and lasted until well after Epiphany.

Favorite saints such as St. Nicholas, St. Christopher, and dozens of others were represented in toy form so that children might mimic their parents by

16

A Neapolitan presepio.

making shrines of their own. Tiny church vessels, candelabra, and crucifixes made of metal, needed to make the settings complete and realistic, were also in demand. Children played with these religious objects with the same serious turn of mind with which they approached dolls and toy furniture when they "played house."

Today, the Christmas crib is becoming a more popular feature as each holiday season approaches. In this how-to-do-it age, many families find it a most engaging pastime to make their own cribs and figures from a wide variety of materials, blending art and craftsmanship, often to a surprising degree. Mass-produced figures and settings are available also, ranging from cheap plaster and papier-mâché to those of expert workmanship. On the other hand, highly creative results are achieved by both amateurs and professionals in the making of Christmas cribs for a more select market. Yet, to many, these religious figurines and the settings that give them their appeal may not seem to fit the category of toys. To be sure, they are not playthings meant for hard play, but rather to be enjoyed for the symbolic message which they convey and for the pictorial effects that they create. In large measure, they take the place of the religious dramas and the peepshows, familiar to earlier generations, and, as many miniature objects, they appeal to all ages. These tiny figures spell out Christmas and its true meaning more vividly than hundreds of words can convey.

In some ways, they resemble the toy theatres. The old tradition of placing the Magi off to one side and moving them a step closer to the manger each day, from Christmas to Epiphany, has great appeal in families where the custom is carried on. Toy historians remind us that the development of cribs in Italy can be compared with that of the doll house of other countries which was popular at the same time. The enthusiasm for cribs was concerned with outdoor settings, whereas interest in the doll house was centered around interiors. The woodcarvers of Oberammergau and the *figurari* of Naples, through their imagination, skill, and artistry, brought new meaning to the simple drama enacted by St. Francis.

"Girl with Hoop," 1850–1860, by an unknown artist. According to *Godey's Lady's Book,* hoops were popular with artists drawing spring fashions for both children and women.

The Abby Aldrich Rockefeller Folk Art Collection

CHAPTER 4

Bring Me a Fairing!

For centuries, "Bring me a fairing" was a familiar request of the children of England, Holland and Russia, Germany, France and Italy, Belgium and Spain, and a dozen little countries now absorbed in the map of modern Europe. "Fairing" was a warmhearted word that could mean almost any kind of toy from most any part of Europe, in the days when the great fairs in the Old World were annual high days and holidays of late summer and autumn. Best of all, a fairing was a trinket or a souvenir, something to amuse, to delight, and to be cherished if it did not break with the using. The country fairs and county fairs which, for more than a century-and-a-half, have delighted America were modeled in many ways after those of Europe.

In the early days of the Christian era, fairs were organized on an elaborate scale by pilgrims who gathered at abbeys and cathedrals on certain feast days to commemorate the saints enshrined there. These great edifices were usually located in open country, removed from villages and towns. As a result, the fair became a community of tents, complete with stalls for selling merchandise and quarters for feeding and lodging the merchants, their helpers, the peddlers who came to buy and sell, and the folk who traveled from afar to attend the fair. Men of all races were included, offering many curious objects ranging from necessities to luxuries. The Feasts of St. James, St. Denis, and especially St. Bartholomew, were important in the English folk calendar. William the Conqueror is said to have granted permission for the first English fair to the Bishop of Winchester. A monk named Rayer, who had been the King's jester, received his charter of Bartholomew Fair, Smithfield, in the year 1133 from King Henry I. The fair became an annual event, until 1855.

Tradition has it that a great fair was in progress in Bethlehem when Mary and Joseph went there for the census. This event and the fact that many native sons were returning to be registered explain why Jesus was born in a stable, since there was no room in the inn. In the time of Constantine, the Roman emperor who established Christianity as the official religion of his Empire, we are told that Jews, Gentiles, and Christians assembled in great numbers to perform religious rites near a tree reputed to have been the famous oak called Mambre under which Abraham, centuries earlier, had received the angels. At the same site, it is recorded that many traders assembled for the sale and purchase of their wares. Thus, from the earliest days of the Christian era, fairs were associated with religious shrines. An old chronicler, writing at the close of the sixth century, complained that his own church was profaned by the public fairs held at the martyrs' shrines. Toy peddlers seem to have made it a practice to gather around the entrances of cathedrals on saints' days and set up their wares in the hope of making sales as the worshippers were leaving after services. Under the Fatimite Caliphs, in the eleventh century, an annual fair was even held on Mount Calvary.

These fairs provided great merriment and social activity for the folk at large, and made possible a pleasant holiday, since they lasted three days. Dancing and rejoicing went hand-in-hand with trading. Entertainment included all the colorful features which we associate with the circus. These were happy times when all ages could enjoy themselves and watch the plays, the side shows, the dancers and the clowns, all the while listening to the cries of the peddlers. In fact, the development of the circus, the origin of the vaudeville show, the rise of the music hall, and the growth of the theater can be traced to these fairs.

Although providing for pleasant recreation, the fair served also as a source of revenue for the maintenance of the church, since licenses were granted and fees paid. There was the day of assembly, the eve of the feast, the feast day, and the following day for packing up, bidding friends good-bye and buying fairings or souvenirs to take home to relatives and friends.

Aside from the pleasure and excitement which the fairs offered, they served as the principal wholesale marketing places for all kinds of goods during the Middle Ages and even up to the time of the Industrial Revolution. Peddlers obtained goods from the merchants and hawked them at the fairs and, later, from door to door through the countryside and in the villages. The wandering peddlers who roamed the countryside, selling notions formerly found in thread-and-needle shops, have been commemorated in costume dolls which date from the middle of the eighteenth century. These peddler dolls, commonly referred to as Notion Nannies, were exceptionally well modeled replicas of the women who were licensed to sell in various parts of England. The cut of her cap, her cape, and her apron were the clues to Nannie's place of origin. Country housewives used to dress these dolls, taking great delight in making and collecting miniatures of the various items which Nannie carried in her tray or basket. They often served as parlor ornaments and were kept under glass domes as curios, to the delight of young and old.

An extraordinary chain of fairs covered the Continent of Europe, to which merchants traveled in great caravans to distribute their goods. To insure their safety, protective leagues were formed which gave them security from highwaymen. The king's "firm peace" was granted to all persons "coming to, staying in, or returning from the fair," which meant that traders were free from arrest, except for any debts arising from traveling. Traders were granted permission to carry swords "not for the hurt of the innocent, but for defense against the robber."

Best known of these protective leagues was the Hanseatic League, which

21

covered the region from as far north as Novgorod in Russia to Bruges, Antwerp, and other cities in Belgium. Other chains of fairs served southern Europe, covering France, Italy, Spain, and other countries.

During the summer months, the merchants who supplied the goods for the various fairs visited the great toy-producing villages of Oberammergau, Berchtesgaden, Thüringen, and other centers to gather their wares. In the eighteenth century, Nuremberg became the great distributing depot for the marvelous hand-carved objects which were made during the winter months. Summer business was brisk in trading, providing food and lodging for the merchants and their helpers, caring for horses, and repairing the vehicles of the caravans.

Trading of this sort created all kinds of business activity. Private homes were converted into inns to accommodate the crowds. The free fairs of the Continent encouraged foreign trade. Tolls were paid to the church, the community, or the person who conferred the royal grant or license. Often when fairs were licensed, local shopkeepers had to close; and sometimes bad weather spelled business ruin for all concerned. These great shifting capitals of trade were highly organized to protect both the buyer and the seller. While cheating did occur, there were strict rules for trading, and violators were punished accordingly. Giving fair weight was a matter of great concern, and tribunals were set up on the fair grounds to see that justice was rendered.

A flourish of trumpets often opened and closed the fair. Music from the melody boxes of organ grinders, the operators of steam pianos, the fiddle, the accordion, and the flute competed with the screams of delight of children who laughed at Punch and Judy or watched a funny man perform. There were freaks too, peddlers galore, all sorts of good things to eat, and toy fairings to take home.

The air was charged with excitement as the crowds moved from stall to stall, gazing in wonder at the latest novelties offered by the peddlers. The spicy fragrance of hot gingerbread, hardly mingling with the oily smell of freshly painted toys, and the presence of too many horses, dogs, and oxen, often brought the familiar barnyard odor too close for comfort. But, it was all a part of the fair, and in this respect fairs have not changed greatly over the years.

Gingerbread figures of the saints, decorated with gilt, were commonplace, as were such trinkets as figurines, hobbyhorses, and various other kinds of toys. Of all the toys associated with fairs, dolls were of prime importance. The term used was poppet, Flanders baby, or Bartholomew baby. Bartholomew babies were elegantly dressed and carefully packed in boxes, and the reference "tricked up with ribbons and bows like a Bartholomew baby" inferred that an eligible young maid who dressed in such a manner would not make a suitable wife, since here was an outlook of "all play and no work."

In the eighteenth century the fair of St. Germain in Paris was the great toy market of France. The fairs held at Nijni Novgorod in Russia and at Leipzig in Germany were also famous for their displays of peasant toys. Henry Cremer, a London toy seller who recorded his observations in a book published in 1873, wrote: "At Easter, the toy merchants from all parts of the
22

Cries of London. Dolls to sell. Green Cabbages Ho.

world meet at the Leipzig Fair; booths, or rather temporary shops, are erected in the principal streets, and these are filled with every novelty in the toy world as well as with old favorites. It is a curious sight to see these toy bazaars, and moreover to see all the hotels in the place plastered with trade cards, and boxes lining the streets in rows, containing announcements on their opened lids."

Whatever the fair, the toys included hobbyhorses, pinwheels, birds on sticks, the "quiz" or "Prince of Wales" toy, the bull roarer, that wonderful noise maker, and many others. Figurines of all sorts included devils, monkeys, song birds, chickens, pretty girls on wire bases that made them wiggle, wooden dolls known as the "penny woodens," toy swings, simple merry-go-rounds, little boats filled with men, wooden animals, and many kinds of jumping jacks, tops, whistles and a dozen other favorites, as well as dolls, plain and fancy. There were fairings for boys and girls, and fairings for sweethearts and wives as well.

Thus, for centuries, in the Old World the children looked forward to these festive days when they could procure, or at least see, new toys. The hawkers and peddlers who traveled from village to village and also set up stalls in the

23

The Punch and Judy Show.

large towns and cities were, likewise, the object of great attention. The Cries of London and Paris recall vividly the colorful personalities who sold all manner of objects from baskets, packs, and trays, or from temporary stalls. These "public characters," the toy seller, the gingerbread man, and the strange fellow who had "young lambs to sell," attracted young and old by their cries and often, because of some peculiarity of appearance, captured the attention and imagination of their prospective customers. The quaint, colorful speeches, verses, and songs they made, and the demonstrations they gave in presenting their wares, were sure-fire for sales.

> Get ready your young lambs to sell! young lambs to sell.
> If I'd as much money as I could tell,
> I'd not come here with young lambs to sell!
>   Dolly and Molly, Richard and Nell,
>   Buy my young lambs, and I'll use you well!

A favorite in the toyman's pack, slung over his shoulder, was the hobby-horse. Sold for a penny or two, it was of simple construction, a stick, two feet or more in length, with a crudely carved horse's head attached. A small flag and two bells gave it additional appeal. A pretty plaything for a "little master," it helped him to imitate the galloping of those real and larger hobbyhorses which he saw in the pageants and mummeries that passed along the streets, or that pranced in the shows at fairs and on the stage. Every child became an actor as he bounced along singing the following ditty, or some variant of it:

24

Ride a cockhorse to Banbury cross,
To see what Tommy can buy;
A penny white loaf, a penny white cake,
And a twopenny apple pie.

In 1892, nearly forty years after the most famous of English fairs had been abandoned, Dr. Henry Morley wrote *Memoirs of Bartholomew Fair*. He painted a lively picture of every aspect of those colorful days as he recalled the cries of the peddlers which Ben Jonson had recorded in his play, *Bartholomew Fair,* written in 1614.

"Buy any ballads! new ballads! Hey?"

Now the Fair's a filling!
O, for a tune to startle
The birds o' the booths here billing,
Yearly with old Saint Bartle!

"Buy any pears, pears, fine, very fine pears!" — "What do you lack, gentlemen? Maid, see a fine hobbyhorse for your young master; cost you but a token a week his provender." (Tokens were farthings coined by tradesmen for

Cries of London. Old Clothes. Young Lambs.

convenience of change, before farthings were issued as King's money by Charles the Second, in 1672.)

"Have you any corns on your feet and toes?"

"Buy a mouse trap, a mouse trap, or a tormentor for a flea?"

"Buy some gingerbread?"

"What do you lack, gentlemen? fine purses, pouches, pin-cases, pipes? What is't you lack? a pair o' smiths to wake you in the morning? or a fine whistling bird?"

"Ballads, ballads! Fine new ballads."

> Hear for your love, and buy for your money.
> A delicate ballad o' the ferret and the coney.
> A Dozen of Divine Points, and the Godly Garters
> The Fairing of Good Counsel, of an ell and three-quarters.

"What do you lack, what do you buy, mistress? A fine hobbyhorse, to make your son a tilter? a drum to make him a soldier? a fiddle to make him a reveller? What is't you lack? Little dogs for your daughters? or babies, male or female?"

CHAPTER 5

The Wonderful World of Dolls

Dolls, the most popular of all toys, have played a role in human history for so long that their origin, like that of the human race, is enshrouded in the mists of antiquity. Practically every archaeological expedition conducted in any part of the world today results in the discovery of some bit of evidence to enable us to piece together the evolution of the doll. To the anthropologist, these discoveries are sometimes of greater import than they are to the layman whose curiosity is generally associated with dolls of more recent origin. While there are numerous stories told about certain kinds of dolls and many romantic fables associated with others, there are still many missing links in the history and lore of the doll.

Who made a particular kind of doll first, and when and where it was made are matters of prime interest to collectors. The comparative rarity of an unusual type is also of significance to those who pursue dolls from the antiquarian point of view. But we need not attempt to tabulate and verify all that has been written, spoken, and conjured up in order to enjoy an old family treasure or the latest handmade item imported from Europe.

Practically all the dolls that have come down to us from the past are females, and even today only about one in twelve manufactured is a male. However, they have never been exclusively girls' toys; boys have always shown an interest in them, and boy dolls are usually thought of as companions for tiny lads. Usually, little boys quickly turn to a favorite stuffed animal which has somewhat the same association for them that a doll has for girls. On the other hand, any little girl will tell you that her dolly means much more than any other toy. Yet, there is more to be said about dolls as playthings, since enjoyment of them is by no means limited to children. For hundreds of years adults have cherished their childhood favorites and preserved them. In many instances, they have spent their mature years collecting various types and kinds of dolls. In fact, there have been periods in history when fads have developed as the result of the introduction of some new kind of doll, sometimes the consequence of a popular children's book.

In his fascinating book *Dolls and Puppets,* Max Von Boehn reminds us that many thousands of years before the doll became a favorite toy it possessed

27

This portrait doll with a bisque head, made about 1900, is believed to be of French origin.

Madeline Merrill Collection

Dimpled china doll of the mid-nineteenth century, considered a rarity by doll collectors.

Mister and Missus dolls of the 1850 period, with heads of papier mache and cloth bodies. In the left foreground, the young lady is made of rawhide, dressed in the style of the 1860's. Her head is of pressed leather, and her body is of cloth.

Madeline Merrill Collection

These two fashionable-lady French dolls of the 1870 era have swivel-neck bisque heads and kid bodies.

Madeline Merrill Collection

"an occult significance with mystical-magical associations which, in an inexplicable way, united the present and the past and reached deep into the world of the unseen." The "board idols," which were made of wood in the Neolithic Age, were sculptured with flat bodies, and these remained typical of the early idols until men learned to model in clay. Some historians have referred to them as the ancestors of the tin soldiers, which were made in Germany centuries later.

Before the dawn of recorded history, dolls were believed to be animate objects, and since the whole of nature is regarded by children and primitive folk as animated, the images of people real or imaginary have had a variety of meanings down through the ages. There was a much-cherished notion in the days of classic antiquity that sculpture in any form was inspired with divine life. Thus, the doll came to have significance as a symbol of power long before it became a plaything for children.

Contrary to popular notions, dolls are not generally found among tribes in the lower cultural levels. In primitive times when dolls were fetishes and idols, their significance was that of either a god or a demon. As Dr. Walter Hough declared, "The evolution of the doll is a very intricate subject. Following the line backward one perceives that dolls lead quickly away from childish hands and become idols; representations in the sense of personations of spiritual or divinized ancestors. Still further back we find images commanded to do the bidding of sorcerers and medicine men; charms, fetishes of sundry sort, household gods, place effigies, objects of witchcraft. Among the most primitive of all are the rude sticks and stones of undeveloped tribes holding crude theories that there is mysterious life in things inanimate, working weal or woe to man.

"A stick or a stone that has been set apart and that by some incantation made to contain more fully the unseen power of the essence of nature is an object dangerously compounded; one to be handled only by those who are initiated. According to early man's idea of supernatural things, particular trees, stones and other objects were saturated, so to speak, with life. The clever medicine men caught this power or some spirit that could do marvelous things and transferred it to a charm or fetish, and of all objects suitable for holding magic power, obviously a human figure of some sort was the best." Thus, dolls were taboo for the children of the tribe, since they represented unseen power.

How did children amuse themselves when the world was young is a question that might well be asked. As Dr. Hough reminds us, "Youngsters in savage tribes found entertainment mainly in the occupations that were destined to be their life work. The girls were taught domestic arts, the boys war and the chase. There were few spare moments for play and loafing. Tribal and family discipline was hard."

The so-called "Venuses" unearthed in France and in the countryside near Vienna, Austria, in recent times, are believed to be among the earliest figurines made by man. However, they bear little resemblance to the classic models of the Goddess Venus carved in marble by Greek sculptors of the Golden Age. These figurines, surviving from the Magdalenian epoch, are more than 25,000 years old. It is believed that they were fetishes used in religious observances,

29

and scholars claim that they are also remote ancestors of the modern doll as we know it.

There is an old story about a group of travelers who once visited Baghdad and presented some women whom they met with dolls for their children. The women looked upon the gifts as spirits and guarded them carefully, being convinced that the dolls would keep their children from harm. In those remote times when dolls were used as ancestor images, they served to represent the loved ones who had passed on. They were revered and worshipped, since it was believed that the spiritual ideals and characteristics of the departed had been transferred to these worshipped forms. Through worship, the images became idols. It was not thought strange to place food and drink before these idols, and pipes for smoking as well.

Among the Romans, ancestor spirits were looked upon as patron gods of the household, which were responsible for the prosperity of the family. Small images, fashioned of wood and highly polished with wax, were placed upon the hearth in the *atrium*. They were allowed to participate in family meals, and small dishes of food were placed before them.

Dolls as playthings were probably first enjoyed by children in Egypt, since remains have been found there in excavated tombs. Centuries earlier, clay images known as "answerers" were in common use in Egypt. These were referred to as servants whose purpose was to accompany the dead on their

Penny Woodens dressed by Miss Margaret Rantoul, Salem, Massachusetts.
Essex Institute Doll Collection

30

Dame Comfort and Family, made by Mrs. Mary Luyster about 1858.
Essex Institute Doll Collection

journey to the spirit world. Curiously enough, these images replaced a strange custom of burying slaves alive with their dead masters.

Although ancient Troy and Crete were famous for their highly developed civilization, the relics of images found there are generally thought to have been idols rather than toys for children. At Athens, on the other hand, in the age of Pericles, five hundred years before the time of Christ, dolls were an integral part of childhood, and some of them had a truly realistic appeal. One of these, still preserved in the University of Pennsylvania, is a diminutive Greek lady with her hair piled high after the fashion of the time, reminiscent in many ways of present-day styles. What is more, she wears a smile so typical of that state of fixed glee seen in modern dolls that, except for visible signs of age, she might be considered the creation of some ultra-smart designer of the twentieth century.

Roman girls, too, had dolls which show evidence of superb workmanship. In *Strange Survivals,* S. Baring Gould, a noted nineteenth-century writer, described a white marble sarcophagus which occupies the center of one of the rooms in the basement of the Capitoline Museum in Rome. "The sarcophagus contains the bones and dust of a little girl, and by the side is the child's wooden doll, precisely like the dolls made and sold today. In the catacombs of St. Agnes one end of a passage is given up to the objects found in the tombs of the early Christians, and among these are some very similar dolls taken out

31

of the graves of the Christian children." Evidence of the practice of burying playthings with a deceased child can be traced back to ancient Egypt, and the widespread belief in this custom, one of those strange survivals that was adopted by the early Christians, has had its parallels even in our own times.

An old tradition associated with dolls in Athens and Rome attests to their importance in family ritual. As they approached maidenhood, having reached the age of discretion, it was the custom for the young ladies to present their dolls for consecration at the Temple of Diana or Venus.

Plato, Aristotle, Horace, Marcus Aurelius, and other great historic figures delighted in marionettes every bit as much as did their children. It has been said that the first child who played with a doll as if it were alive was the originator of the puppet show. Both puppets and marionettes have been popular for so long that their history and development is closely linked with the vagaries of social life of a great part of the world.

The roving entertainers who crossed the Alps with the Roman Legions probably had much to do with popularizing this form of amusement. At any rate, miniature theaters which could be set up at fairs or carried about, or even a few dancing figures who performed to music, proved to be a source of endless fascination for people of all ages until the introduction of movie theaters. Punch and Judy were among the best-loved characters, and as a result of their popularity we think of the show that bears their name synonymously with this type of theater.

In 1321, the Queen of England had a fashion doll imported from France. It became the custom in France to send these miniature mannikins to leading European cities in time to show the latest in fashions for the four seasons. Since dolls have long mirrored the latest in style and dress and the world at large was aware of it, ships carrying these fashion dolls were allowed to pass, even in time of war when all other cargoes were considered contraband. Thus, the Grand Poupée with her hair arranged in the latest mode had a special passport to travel the sea in safety. That fabulous woman, Catherine de Medici, has a niche in doll history as well as in the chronicles of the time in which she lived. An inventory of her property, made after her death, included eight fashion dolls — elaborately garbed in mourning.

Crèche dolls, often seen in museums and antique shops, have a curious kind of appeal. Not only are members of the Holy Family represented in this group, but also men and women in court dress and members of the clergy as well. Some are made entirely of wood, while others have either wax or porcelain heads. Costumes, if original, may be the worse for wear, but they reflect the best in workmanship, often with exquisite detail in tailoring, stitching, and embroidery.

"Penny-woodens" is an endearing name to collectors, for it refers to a simple wooden jointed doll popular in the nineteenth century which could often be bought for a pittance. Some were less than an inch long, while others stood a foot high. They were made in Germany and shipped to many parts of the world. Queen Victoria had a collection of more than a hundred, and Hawthorne described them in *The House of Seven Gables,* referring to the Dutch wooden milkmaids which Hepzibah Pyncheon sold in her cent shop.

32

Uncle Sam, a character doll with a bisque head and jointed composition body, wears his original costume. He was made in Germany in 1890.
Madeline Merrill Collection

This determined lady, made in Germany, is a mid-nineteenth century pegged wooden "Dutch" doll.
Madeline Merrill Collection

An all-wooden, hand-carved English doll of the Empire period with swivel joints, standing 25 inches tall, made about 1800.
Madeline Merrill Collection

This lovely doll has a bisque head and a composition body. Her eyes operate by means of a lever at the back of her head. She was made by Steiner, in France, about 1880.
Madeline Merrill Collection

The pantin, a cardboard figure with movable arms and legs manipulated by strings, became a fashionable toy for adults as well as children in eighteenth-century France.

Essex Institute Doll Collection

Leather, wood, cloth, porcelain, terra cotta, papier-mâché, various kinds of compositions using meal, wax, rubber, fruits like the gourd, flowers like the hollyhock, pine cones, sticks, stones, and odd bits of waste material have provided the raw materials for fashioning dolls. In fact, since there is apparently no limit to human ingenuity, and man quickly learns to make the most of what is at hand, it is not surprising to see distinctive dolls made of such things as pipe cleaners, sea shells, wooden spools, fancy paper, clothespins, and corn husks. Dried apples and pears, when properly treated, make dolls' heads that have all the character marks of truly remarkable faces. The skills involved in making jointed dolls, those with movable eyes and real hair, coupled with all the realistic touches such as the ability to walk, talk, eat and drink, wet the bed, and require a change of clothes, are all a part of the evolution of the best-loved of all toys.

Uncounted numbers of character dolls cherished by private collectors and those assembled in museums around the world are rich in historic association, some of which is well documented. But there is also a wealth of legend, romance and tradition connected with the dolls — all of which adds to the fascination and lure of collecting.

Novelties like Patty Comfort, a hot-water-bottle baby with a celluloid head, patented in 1907, had their vogue and were widely advertised. The body of the doll was a specially shaped hot-water bottle which fitted into a muslin cover. Each doll carried a tag which read:

> Patty Comfort's a rubber lined dolly,
> To hug any other were folly,
> When filled full of air,
> She's light and she's fair
> And filled with hot water she's jolly.

Something truly needed — an unbreakable doll, known as Kathe Kruse, designed by the wife of a noted German sculptor, Professor Max Kruse, was offered to the public in 1910. Many charming dolls, including precious baby types, were originated by this talented woman.

There is something about a rag doll or any homemade toy, that is comfortable, cuddly, and clumsy, which gives it a kind of appeal that no store-toy possesses. The very fact that it is created as an individual piece, or at least requires considerable handwork, even when many are made at a time, attaches to it a personality which no machine quite succeeds in accomplishing. To be sure, many a tiny tot today would have few or no toys if the millions needed to supply our national market depended on the production of the home toy industry.

Those gawky Kewpie dolls we used to see at fairs and carnivals dressed in feathers with cheeks too red and a form too chubby to be quite natural have come a long way in the fair circuits, to remind us that to be "all dressed up like a Bartholomew baby" is no compliment to a woman. For centuries the term has been synonymous with that of an overdressed woman whose spangles and ruffles were indication enough that she would not make a good wife, only a girl given to dancing and rejoicing on "fair" days. This doll was patented by Rose O'Neil about fifty years ago.

35

"Fillette Comique—The Comic Girl." "Amusement with a swinging pendulum figure in many forms." When this young lady is properly balanced she is a most agreeable person, nodding her head in approval for a long time. This nineteenth-century cardboard French toy bears instructions in both German and English.

The Rushford Collections

One of the most interesting links associated with the history of dolls on the North American continent is connected with the ivory dolls of the Eskimos which have been found in the frozen ground on sites where early villages once were located. An old story is known to the inhabitants of the lower Yukon which tells of a doll-being who cut the gut skin that previously covered the holes in the sky. Once openings were made in the firmament, the winds were able to blow across the earth. Eskimo children are told that this doll, which walked on the "path of light," as the Milky Way is called, also performed many generous acts for the people before it passed from life. Thus, the Eskimos showed their gratitude by making dolls for their children, even as the Great Master had made the marvelous doll who bestowed so many benefits upon them.

In recent years the Kachina dolls made by the Hopi Indians of northern New Mexico and Arizona have attracted considerable attention. According to the Hopis, the Kachina is believed to be a supernatural being, whom certain of their men impersonate by wearing masks and elaborate costumes when they perform religious dances. They participate in these ceremonies from the winter solstice through mid-July. When a Hopi man places a mask upon his head and wears the appropriate costume and body paint, he believes that he has lost his personal identity and has received the spirit of the Kachina whom he is supposed to represent. Men take the part of both male and female Kachinas.

Hopi children believe in Kachinas just as our children believe in Santa Claus. As Santa Claus comes at Christmas, bearing gifts to the children, so certain Kachinas bring Kachina dolls, miniature bows and arrows, sweets, fruits, and other food. Thus, Hopi children enjoy a whole series of Christmas delights from late December to July. Kachina dolls are given to the children

36

not as toys, but as objects to be treasured and studied so that the young Hopis may become familiar with the appearance of the Kachinas as part of their religious training. The dolls are taken home, and the parents hang them up on the walls or from the rafters of the house, so that they may be constantly seen by the children of the family and their playmates. Hopi Kachina dolls are neither idols to be worshipped nor icons to be prayed to, but only objects for use in the education of the child.

In 1889, when Thomas Edison presented his experiments with electricity at the Paris Exposition, it seemed as if wonders would never cease. The mechanical marvels of the era of clockwork were surpassed by those of a remarkable American inventor who showed "The Wonders of Electricity" at the Lenox Lyceum in New York City the following year. Edison had invented a phonograph in 1877, and by 1890 the "music machine" was fairly well known, but the miniature theater with twelve dolls on a tiny stage which repeated, each in turn, a verse from Mother Goose, was the highlight of the Exhibition. Although the voices were high-pitched and monotonous, the novelty was more than words could describe. The following year, in a magazine called *The Dolls' Dressmaker,* published by Jenny Wren in New York City, an announcement stated that Edison's talking doll, described as "the greatest wonder of the age," sold for twenty dollars, dressed. *The Scientific American* notified its readers that the factory which made these dolls was equipped to turn them out at the rate of five hundred a day.

One of the most highly cherished dolls in the Smithsonian Institution in Washington, D. C., is a colorfully dressed Breton peasant presented by the children of Brittany to General Dwight D. Eisenhower in gratitude for the part he played in the liberation of France in World War II.

The significance and sentiment of a doll which appeared in the October, 1869, issue of *Godey's Lady's Book* has not changed, even in the space age. Victor Hugo wrote this appraisal in *Les Miserables:* "A doll is one of the most imperious wants, and at the same time one of the most delicious instincts, of feminine childhood. To clean, clothe, adorn, dress, undress, dress again, teach, scold a little, nurse, lull, send to sleep, and imagine that something is somebody — the whole future of a woman is contained in this. While dreaming and prattling, making little trousseaux and cradles, while sewing little frocks and aprons, the child becomes a girl, the girl becomes a maiden, and the maiden a woman. The first child is a continuation of the last doll."

The story of dolls is an endless tale so closely interwoven with every facet of the romance of toys that allusions to them appear in nearly every chapter of a book such as this. Therefore, no attempt has been made to marshal all the pieces of the doll picture-puzzle into this chapter. Nor is this essay more than a glimpse into the doll world. Historians and avid collectors have told the story in a variety of ways, and the reader who would pursue the subject of dolls in all its ramifications will find the bibliography a useful guide.

Doll house and furnishings, made in 1852 for the children of Annie
Crowninshield Warren.

Essex Institute Collection

CHAPTER ⑥

The Romance of Doll Houses

A doll house is more than a mere toy. It is history in a capsule, a mosaic, an eyeful of the past, a catalog of pictures, or even a three-dimensional record that tells more of a given era than thousands of words can convey. For four hundred years or more, this curiosity of the toy world has captured the imagination of folk of all ages in Europe, America, and the Orient. Yet, in the toy world, it is a newcomer. In practically every era some ingenious individual, and, at times, several, have designed and built doll houses that merited recognition as works of art. Of the notable examples that remain, some are so highly treasured in museums that they are encased in glass to assure their preservation. How vividly they convey to us, with a kind of magic, the mode of life and the whims of fashion in other days. They fill us with a sense of enchantment and wonder, as we marvel at the meticulous care with which every little detail has been executed. The world of Lilliput in *Gulliver's Travels* is much easier to visualize because of them. Of one thing we can be certain — when children played with them, it was gentle play. Otherwise, these fragile gems would have disappeared long since, as has been the fate of most toys.

Carl Gröber, the noted German toy historian, has focused attention on another aspect of the doll house. "Nothing can give a clearer picture of the wealth of objects produced for the joy, amusement, and instruction of children than the doll's house or room; for here in almost bewildering profusion has been brought together all that has been produced in the nature of playthings." The ingenuity, imagination, and extraordinary skill required to make the fittings of a doll house have always been as apparent to a child as they were to a parent, but each expressed it differently. Things in miniature have seldom required more than an expression of delight to convey what they meant. Doll houses say it with nostalgia.

Essentially, the early doll houses were luxury toys, and the most elaborate structures were obviously made by highly skilled craftsmen who lavished all their talent on these miniature houses. Each had a stamp of individuality which is evident even in those of rather crude construction made by doting fathers or the hired man. When produced in quantity, as they have been

39

during the past several decades, these toy houses had to be simplified in detail and in design, because of cost and shipping problems. Somehow, those made of cardboard lack the "real" touch of the wooden houses, however charming and well designed they were. A fair number of early examples remain in good condition. In Europe, the term "doll's house," rather than "doll house," is commonly used and, in earlier centuries, it was "baby house."

Other toys which belong in this category are the Noah's arks, the toy theaters, the Christmas cribs, the doll rooms, the toy kitchens typified in the fabulous Nuremberg type, and various kinds of miniature shops and markets. All fit into the picture, since they are creations of architectural and scenic significance. These fabulous toys convey to us a sense of the importance of detail and the fascination of observing the minutiae of life. Somehow, these playthings "in little" are prime proof of that old adage that "it is the little things in life that count."

Like the doll, the doll house, and particularly its furnishings, played an important part in the world of fashion; that is, in furnishing trends in homes. Some were made expressly as drummers' samples to be carried about in the days before catalogs were issued. In like manner, a considerable part of the so-called child's furniture of earlier days belongs in this category. Easily handled, these miniatures were carried either on the backs of the walking salesman or in packs strapped to horses, or in wagons.

Those treasured relics of Egyptian, Greek, and Roman culture, miniatures in metal, ivory, and wood, such as a tiny ivory bed found in the Temple of Hera at Olympia in Greece, may have been used in doll houses of ancient times. Among the toy treasures in New York's Metropolitan Museum of Art is a folding bed, made of wood, about a foot long, with six legs, two of which fold. It even has a headboard and the spring, which has been restored, is of string. Perhaps a leather thong was used originally. This piece of furniture dates back a thousand years before the time of Christ. There is also a curious jointed figure on a board, with a string attached, dated 2000 B.C. When the cord is pulled, the figure moves, as if kneading bread. Other relics of what could be considered as doll's furniture have been found, and the children of ancient times may have had miniature houses as toys. But to put all the parts of the puzzle together was not easy, since the items were small and fragile.

During the early part of the Christian era, and in fact throughout the Middle Ages, we find few references to toys of any kind. Actually, the fragments of toys found in more ancient cultures make it easier for scholars to trace the development of playthings in everyday life at that time than in the first ten centuries of modern history.

As with most toys of wood displaying top craftsmanship, the doll house had its origin in Germany, but the fashion soon spread to Holland, Belgium, France, England, the Scandinavian countries and, in fact, wherever ornate toys were enjoyed.

A doll house attributed to Bavaria in 1558, believed to be the earliest on record, was made at the request of Duke Albrecht for his little daughter, but it has not survived. After the meticulous custom of those times, careful inventories were made, and from the inventory we learn of its splendor, and can visualize what it must have looked like.

40

Many of these early doll houses resembled china cabinets or curio cases. The rooms, arranged on several levels, were protected by glass. The moldings, framework, and bases often were inlaid elaborately. Every piece of furniture, footstool, bedstead, table or cupboard, was fashioned by the most accomplished of cabinet makers. Silver, kitchen utensils, china, fabrics, rugs and, in fact, every item of the décor, bore the mark of craftsmanship. There was about the furnishings a quality that made one marvel at their beauty and their perfection. The vanity of the owner was sometimes expressed by the presence of his portrait in miniature. In fact, many of the cabinets, made in Holland, were so ornate that historians are not certain whether they were made for children or for the delight of wealthy Dutch burghers, just as automatons were made in France during the reign of the Louis's for the delight of the Court. As the popularity of doll houses increased, during the seventeenth and eighteenth centuries, they became a most engaging pastime, reaching, in some instances, the status of a craze with those who had the time and the money to indulge their whims.

At the University of Upsala, in Sweden, there is a most remarkable house in the form of a cabinet which was purchased from a great German craftsman in 1637 as a gift to Gustavus Adolphus, King of Sweden. Perhaps the best-known doll-house story concerns Peter the Great of Russia. He was visiting in Holland when the craze was at its height, and ordered a cabinet made. When the house was completed five years later, the cost exceeded the 20,000-florin estimate, so he refused it. Thus, it remained in Holland. Another version has it that a retired merchant made doll cabinets for his own amusement and gave them away to friends and museums. Peter admired his work, and the merchant offered to make him one. He labored for twenty-five years, and, when finished, he sent word to Peter, who asked what he owed for the masterpiece. The merchant was so offended that he replied that "even a Czar had not money enough to pay for twenty-five years of a man's life," and he presented the doll house to the nation.

Individual dolls' rooms were also an outgrowth of this fashionable and popular trend. In 1630, Cardinal Richelieu presented an elaborate room with six dolls to the little daughter of a friend, Princesse d'Enghien. She found great pleasure in dressing and undressing the dolls, but was not permitted to bathe them, since they were so delicate that water would have damaged the faces and bodies.

As time passed, the rage for doll houses continued, and eventually they became popular among children everywhere. While most of them could not expect to possess the ornate houses which the landed gentry sported, they found pleasure in home-made structures fashioned from crates and boxes, or arranged in simple cabinets and cupboards. Dickens described a doll house with all the enthusiasm of a child. Kate Greenaway wrote of them for later audiences, and told how she collected miniatures of Queen Victoria and the royal family, and all the furniture to go with them. In Victoria's day, everyone knew that she had played with dolls until she was fourteen (she was Queen at seventeen), that she made the clothes for thirty or more of her great collection, and that she had a doll house, too. What the Queen had and loved set the fashion of the day for young and old.

Interior view, Vaughan dollhouse.
Essex Institute Collection

Miniature kitchen utensils, tea sets, and every conceivable kind of practical and ornamental object "in little" have been made for centuries, but usually the early pieces were individually made or produced in small quantities by craftsmen. However, with the rise of the toy-making industry in both Europe and America, great quantities of these delightful toys were turned out. The same is true of doll's furniture, with its slavish adherence to popular trends, good, bad, and indifferent as far as taste is concerned. Aside from the pleasure which these toys provided when they were produced, the remnant that survives serves as a reminder of all-but-forgotten fads in furnishings.

Of all the toy rooms, none could surpass the Nuremberg kitchens for charm in true Lilliputian fashion. To describe them is to waste words, for they must be seen and played with as they were by German children and those of other countries to which they were shipped in the late eighteenth and nineteenth centuries. Playing house with such a kitchen, a little girl could not help but learn what each utensil was for and "what belonged where." There was a place for everything in these miniature rooms.

Shops of all kinds, operated by such tradespeople as the milliner, the grocer, the butcher, the seedsman, the baker, the florist, the hardware merchant, the toy seller, and ever so many more, all replete with tiny wares, made the best of toys. They were referred to as "bazaars" and provided a most convenient way to display one's collection of miniatures. In fact, they had all the

42

charm of the "pedlar dolls" or "Notion Nannies" that reposed on a table in the parlor.

The twentieth-century doll houses owned by the late Queen Mary of England and by Colleen Moore, noted American actress of World War I fame, had their counterpart in one made at the request of a German spinster in 1631. Anna Köferlin loved children and made a doll house for public exhibition, and published a pamphlet about it. She told how a household of her day should be arranged and cared for when she wrote, "as to the education of girls, I must make mention of the toys with which many played until they became brides; namely, the so-called dolls' houses."

Queen Mary, wife of George VI, was the owner of what is considered the most fabulous doll house ever made. It was designed by Sir Edward Luytens, one of England's noted architects, and built in the 1920's. Three books were published to describe this remarkable structure, and all are exceedingly scarce. They are *The Book of the Queen's Dolls' House,* in two volumes, one of which discusses the house and the other the extraordinary library which the house contains. Later, there appeared a condensation called *Everybody's Book of the Queen's Dolls' House,* from which we have this graphic description: "The House itself is 100 inches long on its main north and south fronts, and 62 inches from east to west. It stands on a base 116 inches by 72 inches and 39 inches high. This base is divided into two parts. The lower 24 inches contains 208 interchangeable drawers, half on the north and half on the south, covered by falling flap doors. Each door is 11¼ inches long, and 3½ inches wide and deep, made of cedar and fitted with a drop ring handle of ivory . . . The upper 15 inches of the base contains the machinery, the electric transformers, the switches, the tank for bath wastes, the wine cellar and storeroom for groceries, both ample and suitably victualled. In this part of the base also are two very charming surprises. At the west end a flap falls down, a drawer extends, and, behold, there is a complete garage, with six tiny motorcars, with an inspection pit in the painted brick paving, and with everything to invite the interest of midget mechanicians! At the east a similar transformation allows a lovely garden to be extended on double runners, so as to display its exquisite imitations."

On April 14, 1924, this extraordinary doll house made headlines on the front page of the *New York Times.* "Drys Protest Wine Cellars in Queen Mary's Doll House. People aroused to indignation by the discovery that Queen Mary's million-dollar doll house has wine cellars containing miniature cases of champagne, whiskey and other alcoholic beverages which they say no self-respecting doll would drink or even have in the house." The rest of the story is told in the final paragraph of the dispatch, "Protests have been made, but without results, and Her Majesty's exquisitely furnished replica of an English home, wine cellars and all, will be on view at the Wembley exhibition . . ."

This house is as intriguing to look at as it is to read about. Not only are the details of construction, the equipment, and the furnishings intriguing, but every room, including the fabulous library, offers its share of surprises. The garage, with its fleet of limousines, 1924 style, and its tiny motorcycles, the plumbing, lighting, the two elevators — one for the family and the other for

the servants — the fanciful garden, complete even to tiny snails and birds' eggs — these and scores of other unbelievably small minutiae are there to dazzle and to delight all who see it.

Colleen Moore built a castle which is now housed in the Chicago Museum of Science and Industry. It, too, was the subject of a book, but a much more modest volume than that published about Queen Mary's treasure. For many years, Miss Moore's castle was exhibited throughout the country, and often attracted 100,000 visitors in a single day. Money for admissions was given to charity, and the castle itself is reported to have cost a million dollars. This is the kind of doll house to delight small children who are still passing through that glorious world of fantasy peopled by Mother Goose, Little Jack Horner, Jack and Jill, Little Bo-Peep, Hansel and Gretel, and the knights of King Arthur, for they are all here, along with a dozen more of those rare creatures who inhabit the story books in the world of make-believe. Created in the spirit and atmosphere of Hollywood, with all its glitter and glamour, this castle was the culmination of a natural expression of love for doll houses which dated back to Miss Moore's girlhood. At the age of two, her father made her first doll house, and she had seven, in all, during her lifetime.

Stories galore have been written about the castle and many of them make as good reading as the fairy tales she has dramatized so skillfully. Her jewels have been incorporated in the chandelier, which is suspended from the drawing-room ceiling. Diamonds, emeralds, and pearls were taken from four bracelets, a ring, and two necklaces to complete it. There are eleven rooms, including a strange room with a mural of Ali Baba and a chapel containing an organ operated by water and electricity. The ivory floor of the chapel "is symbolic of events from the Old Testament, telling the story of the Lamb of God, the Dove of Peace, the Ram, the Locusts, and the Years of Plenty. In the great center design are the Ten Commandments as hewn in the tablets. The Lights of the World shine forth in hues of purple and gold. The stained-glass windows by Brabon depict originals and copies of famous masterpieces of David and Goliath, Moses in the Bulrushes, Daniel in the Lions' Den, and the Judgment of Solomon.

Flora Gill Jacobs, who has devoted many years to the pursuit of doll-house lore, wrote of it in *A History of Doll Houses:* "Since her treasures have been both found and commissioned all over the world, there are innumerable anecdotes about their acquisition, some of them extraordinary. One has to do with Cinderella's glass slippers, which Miss Moore felt belonged in her doll house. And she wanted them hollow; however small Cinderella's feet may have been, even she could not have got into slippers which weren't hollow. No glass blower seemed to think the feat possible. Miss Moore went so far as Venice. But even the famed makers of Venetian glass shook their heads. She came home and found a retired glass blower in Jackson, Michigan, willing at least to try. The slippers, somewhat over a quarter of an inch long, with high heels and red glass bows, are now among the museum pieces in the princess's drawing room.

"In its early years, the doll house inspired almost a toy industry of its own. All sorts of Colleen Moore playthings were made, most of them relevant to

Interior of the Vaughan dollhouse at the Essex Institute, Salem, Massachusetts.

doll housing; such matters as 'doll house food and dishes — breakfast, lunch, and dinner — baking sets.' The most impressive of these sidelines was more than a toy; color movies of the castle, with sound, a series of six films. For part of this, the castle's owner recorded her own description. Two films anticipated the recent Disney blend of photograph and animation: in these a prince and princess, acting as host and hostess, escorted the fairyland characters around the premises."

The Doll Festival, held in Japan each year in March and sometimes referred to as the Peach Blossom Festival, may seem to have no connection with the story of doll houses. Yet, this charming observance has the kind of setting that one finds in a doll house, even though it is specially improvised for the occasion. Best described as a ceremonial tableau, it involves ancient customs relating to dolls that symbolize Japanese ancestor worship. At the same time, it provides parents with a means of expressing their "love for their children, their joy and pride in them, and their desire to please them," as Tomatsu Iwadō has expressed it in *Children's Days in Japan*. The association with peach blossoms in this land steeped in symbolism dates back to the time when the moon was the determining factor in the Japanese calendar. Peaches bloomed in the third month, hence the name.

Established in the eighteenth century by the Shōgun Yoshimune for the pleasure of his large family of girls, this festival is a most significant part of family life. The dolls used are not the everyday kind with which children play, but rather the family ceremonial dolls, or heirlooms, which have been

45

handed down from generation to generation. Usually a set consists of at least fifteen dolls. Present custom dictates their arrangement on either five or seven shelves. On the top shelf, the Prince is placed on the left, and the Princess on the right. Dressed as members of the Imperial Court used to be in olden times, the costumes which the dolls wear resemble those used at present-day ceremonials in Japan. A folding screen of gold forms the background for the shelves, with lanterns flanking the sides. In the center there is a tray on which a festooned sacred tree is placed.

On the second shelf three maids of honor stand, ready to serve saké. The third shelf is occupied by five musicians, each holding an instrument, while the fourth holds a pair of guardsmen, and the fifth three footmen. To this array are added the favorite dolls with which the girls play each day.

A party-like atmosphere pervades the whole house as trays filled with red and blue confetti-like sweets are placed near the dolls' court. Lozenge-shaped rice cakes are arranged on a pair of trays, and small tables in pairs are brought in to hold the rice bowls, side bowls, soup bowls, and the inevitable chopsticks with which to eat the delicacies.

The colorful setting is further enhanced by a tiny cherry tree and a tiny orange tree, both in full bloom, which are placed on either side of the footmen on the lowest shelf. Artificial cherry blossoms, arranged as a flowering ball, and another of orange blossoms are hung from the ceiling, each with a long silken cord trailing from it.

The Doll Festival is never complete without "white saké," which is served in tribute to the dolls and for the pleasure of the family and all the visitors who take part in the celebration. Since this drink is noted for its potency, it is served to the children in very small amounts. In recent years, this festival of many meanings has generated great interest among girls in countries around the world, with the result that leading museums feature displays of Japan's Doll Festival.

CHAPTER

The Marvelous Era of Automatons

Fantasy in toyland is everywhere we look, but nowhere is it more apparent than in the realm of mechanical toys. The dancing man, the singing bird, the piano player, the walking doll — these and hundreds of other playthings that move as if they were alive have been a source of enjoyment to young and old for centuries. Long before the Christian era, mechanical devices imbued men with a feeling of awe and wonder. The spectacles which these automatons created in the courts of Europe during the period following the Renaissance were equally remarkable but, for the most part, the opportunity to see them perform was limited to royalty and to those who frequented the palaces and great houses. Occasionally public exhibitions were held, and these became notably popular in the eighteenth century. A hundred years later, when clockwork toys were made in quantity, nearly everyone was able to afford them. Yet their appeal to human fancy was as strong as it had been centuries earlier in ancient Greece, where nearly every household had its favorite mechanical toy, or in Alexandria, where reaction to the intriguing objects had often been one of wonder mixed with fear.

In today's age of jet propulsion, these extraordinary creations designed by long-forgotten inventors, ranging from ancient times to the end of the nineteenth century, seem rather commonplace. Now, even the most unusual developments in mechanical toys amuse rather than excite us. Surrounded as we are by daily accounts of Space-Age activities in newspapers, radio, and television, we can hardly marvel at them as did our forefathers. Yet, as we turn the pages of history and read of the automatons of bygone days, we can readily understand why they were so much discussed and why they gave rise to so many fantastic tales. No present-day fishing enthusiast — even in his wildest dreams — could possibly conjure up stories like some of the fables that were told about the curious automatons. However, not all the comments made were entirely complimentary to their producers.

Marionettes, unlike automatons, were controlled by strings which were plainly visible and easily handled. These presented no sense of mystery, nor even the slightest suggestion of sorcery, since they depended merely on the guidance of a skilled manipulator. But a kind of magic which could be sus-

Banjo player, made by Jerome Secor, shakes his head, plunks the banjo and taps his feet, all with a few turns of the key.
The Rushford Collections

When Mammy is wound up, she tosses the "China head" darling in the air with rather agitated affection.
The Rushford Collections

pect — or so it seemed to many folk at the time — was created by the skilled artisans who used air, water, mercury, and clockwork — all invisible to the eye — to operate their mechanical devices. As a consequence, the more realistic and life-like the mechanical object, the greater became the possibility of its creator being accused of traffic with Satan. And, not a few of the early mechanicians were denounced, and even punished, for their daring feats.

A soaring mechanical eagle that greeted the Emperor Maximilian at Nuremberg in 1470 had its counterpart in a lumbering lion, devised by no less a person than Leonardo da Vinci in 1509 for Louis XII's reception in Milan. Descartes, the noted French scientist, Roger Bacon, Louis XIV, Queen Victoria, and Ravel, the composer, and many other distinguished figures in various countries of the world had a flair for mechanical figures. The attention given to them by so many prominent persons paved the way for a craze that stirred court circles to a high pitch of excitement in the seventeenth and eighteenth centuries. Eventually, a great industry developed which absorbed mechanics and even court jewelers, who vied with one another in producing novelties of great distinction.

Back in 400 B.C., Archytas of Tarentum had made a wooden pigeon that would fly, and this invention was the talk of the Old World. The body of the bird was filled with air which, as it gradually escaped, caused the bird to move. Singing birds, produced by the ingenious Arabs and the scholars of Alexandria, were thought of as amazing. But some looked upon them as works of the Devil. A metal fly that buzzed across a room, circled around the chairs of a group of startled guests and returned to rest on its maker's hand, had all of Germany agog in the late 1400's. The same inventor captured the fancy of Maximilian in 1470

48

when he let loose a mechanical eagle, which traveled some distance from the city of Nuremberg to meet the distinguished visitor and then returned to perch at the gates of the city until the great leader arrived.

The story of Leonardo da Vinci's lion, constructed in 1509 for Louis XII's reception in Milan, is another fantastic tale. When the King was seated on his throne, da Vinci placed the animal on the floor at the opposite end of the great hall. It moved slowly toward the King, stopped in front of him, and, as if in humble tribute, tore open its chest with its claws. Fleurs-de-lis, the symbol of the French royal house, tumbled out and fell at the King's feet.

Descartes had a theory that all animals, including man, were merely highly developed machines. To prove it, he built a mechanical figure of a young girl whom he called Ma Fille Franchina. Shortly after he had finished his model, Descartes took her with him on a sea voyage, during which time the ship's captain set her in motion, either from curiosity or by accident. At any rate, the bewildered sea captain became so upset that he tossed the mechanical girl overboard, believing that she was surely the work of the Devil. How much of this story is fact is difficult to ascertain, but even as a bit of tradition, or just as a good yarn, it relates to a period when the construction of automatons was absorbing the attention of scientists everywhere in the Old World.

Less than a century after Descartes' death, Pierre Jacquet-Droz, a Swiss watchmaker, and his son Henri Louis, who died at the height of his fame in 1790, gained fame for their mechanical creations. Both father and son were ranked among the most skillful of all producers of automatons. Pierre's parents possessed more than an ordinary income and, realizing their son's desire for study, had planned since his early childhood for his career as a preacher. While he was enjoying a holiday from theological school, he visited his sister, who had married a watchmaker. He was so fascinated by mechanics that he forsook religion for watchmaking. In 1752, at the age of thirty-one, he made his first singing bird, a tiny object which he placed in a gold snuff box so that it would pop out like a jack-in-the-box when the cover was removed.

Six years later the King of Spain commissioned him to make various kinds of mechanical objects. These proved to be so extraordinary and lifelike that he was almost condemned as a *sorcier* at the time of the Inquisition. Later he sent his son, Henri, to the University of Nancy to study mathematics, in order to further perfect the skill which he wished to pass on to his heir. Later both father and son, in company with Jean Pierre-Droz, created several automatons which brought them world-wide fame. When Henri took control of the business, he opened a branch in London and was received by George III. Later, when he visited Paris, Louis XVI and Marie Antoinette invited him to appear at Court. Interest was keen in the remarkable automatons that this famous firm had created. Among them were "The Young Writer," "The Designer," or "The Artist," as it was sometimes called, and "The Clavecin Player." "The Clavecin Player" rendered a minuet in so real and lifelike a manner that all who viewed it marvelled at the fact that it was entirely mechanical. All are preserved today in perfect working order in the Museum at Neuchatel, Switzerland, where Pierre was born.

Mechanical figures were by no means new, but Pierre Jacquet-Droz had the rare skill of producing models that were not only masterpieces of mechanical skill, but which were also noted for a precise kind of workmanship and finish that had not been seen previously.

"The Writer," his first effort, represents a young child seated on a stool before a desk. When put into motion, the little model dipped his pen in the ink, shook off the surplus with a most natural gesture, and proceeded to write clearly and carefully. Initials were properly placed, and the space between words was as thoughtfully planned as if a skilled writer were at the desk. As each line was completed, the little hand held the pen and moved it back again to the beginning of the next line. Even more amazing was the fact that all the while the performance was taking place, the eyes of the little fellow were fixed on his work, simulating with complete naturalness the actions of a young child writing. After a word was written, the writer would cast a glance at a sheet or letter nearby, from which it appeared to be copying. No wonder it was considered so remarkable!

"The Musician," made by Henri Louis, was the largest of the mechanical toys, measuring nearly six feet in height. At the time, there was no mechanism in existence that sounded like a piano. The musician, a charming figure of a young girl with long, slender fingers, was seated at a harpsichord, or an early type piano, with her hands outstretched. When the mechanism was wound, the figure leaned forward to be nearer the keyboard, moving her body in the typical emotional way of a performer and played an old French melody with all the flourishes of an accomplished artist.

"The Designer," or "Draughtsman," drew sketches which were lacking somewhat in detail and finish, but the likeness astounded everyone. As with an artist studying his model, the automaton paused from time to time as he sketched, examined his work, corrected mistakes and even blew the eraser dust from the paper. When the drawing was completed, the courtiers gathered around the mechanical artist and were astonished to find that he had produced a portrait of their King crowned with a wreath of laurel. Later, when Henri Louis gave a demonstration at the English court, the automaton drew a portrait of the English monarch. Such an accomplishment more than piqued the curiosity of all who witnessed it. The childhood spirit of awe and wonder was more prevalent in court than in the nursery.

Such toys were costly and had to be handled with the greatest of care, but even at this time less complicated playthings were being made for children. Craftsmanship and skill were lavished on children's theaters, animated with tiny moving figures, sedan chairs borne aloft by swarthy servants, carriages with tiny concealed clockwork, drawn by teams of miniature horses, and entire regiments of toy soldiers that marched with the greatest precision.

A clock is hardly a toy in any sense of the word, since its prime purpose is to tell time — but a musical clock has all the fascination of a toy, and it can be enjoyed by young and old alike. Both Pierre and Henri Jacquet-Droz earned great fame for their clocks. One of their most unusual timepieces was presented to their patron, Ferdinand VI of Spain. The gift was made before the assembled Court. This remarkable clock, which played nine tunes, had many unusual features. Part of the elaborate ornamentation included a lady seated on a balcony who waved her hand and nodded her head, all the while keeping time with

50

Walking doll and carriage, patented by William F. Goodwin, 1868.
Essex Institute Doll Collection

the music. She paused to take an occasional pinch of snuff, and when the glass door of the clock was opened, she bowed politely. In addition, there was a shepherd who played a flute, a lamb who made a bleating cry, and a dog who stood watch over a basket of miniature apples. If anyone touched the fruit, he would bark. Here, indeed, was a man-made marvel that was so real as to be unbelievable. Pierre was proud indeed of his achievement, and informed the King that the much-admired dog was as faithful as he was well-behaved. He then urged the monarch to test the dog by touching the fruit. When Ferdinand reached forward to take one of the apples, the dog moved his head toward him so naturally that a puppy in the room began to bark.

Terrified by the apparent sorcery, the courtiers made a speedy exit, leaving behind the King and his Naval Minister. Pierre then requested the minister to ask the shepherd for the correct time, but no reply came from the automaton. Then it was that the great craftsman made the casual remark that the herdsman was probably not familiar with Spanish. The minister responded by asking for the time in French, and to his astonishment the shepherd answered him at once.

One of the most fabulous creations of the eighteenth century was made by a German baron in 1776. This was an automatic chess player, dressed as a life-

51

Autoperipatetikos or Walking Doll, wound with a key. Patented in 1862 by Joseph Lyon & Co. The doll has a china head and kid arms.

Essex Institute Doll Collection

sized Turk. It toured Europe from St. Petersburg to London, thrilling spectators with its performance, and it was not until 1789, six years after it appeared in London, that a book published in Dresden revealed it to be a hoax. A well-trained boy, exceedingly thin and tall for his age, was concealed in a drawer below the chess board and made possible the skilled operations of the chess player.

Louis XIV was the recipient of a miniature carriage, the work of Dr. Camus, an associate of the French Academy of Sciences. Drawn by a team of horses, it had a coachman, a footman, a page, and a lady passenger. When Dr. Camus brought it to the palace, he placed it at one end of a long table and set it in motion for the pleasure of the King and his Court. The story is told that when the coachman cracked his whip the horses moved forward so realistically that children present were startled, for they believed the tiny animals were alive. When the carriage had traveled the length of the table the horses made a sharp turn and continued until they arrived in front of the King, where they halted. Then the footman and page stepped down, opening the carriage door so that the lady might alight to curtsy and present a petition to the astonished Louis. After waiting a moment, she curtsied again and re-entered the carriage, the servants resumed their positions, and the vehicle moved on.

Jewels and precious metals were used in profusion by the skilled craftsmen whose task it was to create more and more novelties of this type for the delight of royalty and their families. The exquisite detail of the embellishments was exceeded only by the minuteness of the mechanisms concealed in ornamented rings, brooches, and watches. Science and art were linked in an age when elegance and novelty were the order of the day.

Jacques de Vaucanson, who was born in France at the beginning of the eighteenth century, gave his long life to the production of mechanical toys. He became famous for many kinds of performing artists whose movements were natural and lifelike. One of his most celebrated achievements was a mechanical duck that paddled through the water seeking food. The creature swallowed grain, digested it, and disposed of it in a natural manner. It also swam, preened its feathers, and moved its neck. Tradition has it that a French sailor who fought at Trafalgar used his inventive mind to simplify the elaborate mechanism of de Vaucanson and made possible the production of inexpensive toys that were to become popular in Europe and America in Victorian days.

Napoleon and the Empress Josephine showed keen enthusiasm for mechanical toys, and it is recorded that Josephine spent considerable time collecting and enjoying the latest novelties which the skilled craftsmen of France were turning out at the time. She is also credited with using them as gifts to please the children who came to visit her. Even the poor who came begging food and money went away with some amusing plaything from the Empress' collection. Queen Victoria had her favorites, too, among these lively toys. At an early date, long before cheap mechanical toys were produced in quantity for the American market, some of the best produced in France, Germany and Switzerland found their way to the United States. These were cherished treasures indeed, brought back to children by the captains of the square riggers who sailed to distant ports from the Eastern seaboard.

CHAPTER 8

Adventures in Toy Valley

Three centuries ago German woodcarvers, working with simple tools and the wood from nearby forests, found the key to children's hearts all over the world when they began to make toys as a home industry. Many a German village could have been called "Toy Town," "Toy Land," "Toy Valley," or "The Wonderland of Childhood," for such was the nature of communities like Oberammergau, Berchtesgaden, and Erzgebirge, and regions like Thüringia and the Gröden Valley in South Tyrol. Since the turn of the present century the name "Toy Town" has been linked inseparably with St. Ulrich, the toy center of the Gröden Valley, and the valley itself has been the subject of many delightful stories. Among these is one written for children by Margaret Warner Morley, *Donkey John of the Toy Valley.* Long brown barns, several stories high, with galleries running completely around them where grain was hung to dry and carvers exposed their freshly cut pine to the weather, add a picturesque quality to the prosperous town of St. Ulrich. This area is also famous as a ski and winter sports resort.

Ever since the Middle Ages, craftsmen in Europe have been organized in guilds. Toy makers working with wood and metal belonged to different guilds, depending on the type of work they performed. A worker skilled in wood carving was a specialist who devoted all his energies to his craft. Painting was a similar skill, and so, too, was working with metal. It was a case of each to his own skill, and regulations did not permit craftsmen to do more than one kind of work. Whatever the craft, work was done in homes or small workshops on the property. Often father and the older boys who were learning a skill were assisted by mother and the girls of the family. Each and every member of the family acquired a special technique.

In the Gröden Valley it was not uncommon to see an old woman sitting on a slope, whittling toys while tending her cows; or a child seated at the door of a cottage, carving a tiny animal from a block of pine, was a common sight. Prior to World War I, three out of every five inhabitants in this valley were engaged in toy making.

Whether the wooden toy was a doll or an animal, the process of fashioning it was the same. When dolls were being made, one member of the family carved

54

the head, another the body, and still another the legs and arms. Sometimes, still another craftsman and his family assembled the dolls. Then the toys were sent to a third craftsman to be painted. For many years, the carvers in the Gröden Valley sent all their toys to Oberammergau to be painted.

Carving became a traditional skill to be passed on from one generation to another, so that the quality of even the so-called "cheap" toys was stamped with the individuality of the maker to a surprising degree, despite the mechanical way in which they were produced.

More than sixty years ago, Amelia B. Edwards described this tradition in *Untrodden Peaks and Unfrequented Valleys,* and as a result induced travelers to seek out these remote villages where craftsmanship was a coveted art. She has given us an unforgettable picture of "an old, old woman at work, Magdalena Paldauf by name. She carved cats, dogs, wolves, sheep, goats, and elephants. She has made these six animals her whole life long, and has no idea of how to cut anything else. She makes them in two sizes and she turns out, as nearly as possible, a thousand of them every year. She has no models or drawings of any kind to work by; but goes on steadily, unerringly, using gouges of different sizes, and shaping out her cats, dogs, wolves, sheep, goats, elephants, with an ease and an amount of truth to nature that would be clever if it were not so utterly mechanical. Magdalena Paldauf learned from her mother how to carve these six animals, and her mother had learned it in a like manner from her grandmother. Magdalena has now taught the art to her own granddaughter; and so it will go on being transmitted for generations."

Nuremberg gave the wooden toys their trade name, for it became the great distributing depot for the rural and village toy makers in the eighteenth century. Children everywhere heard their wooden playthings referred to as "Nuremberg toys." Here the agents assembled the finished toys and supervised their sale and distribution to the world. Since Nuremberg was geographically well situated, it was a logical and natural distribution center for the industry. Then too, it became also a great production center for tin soldiers and other metal toys and, like Germany itself, was thought of as the toy cupboard of the world.

The peasants who lived in the heavily wooded forest areas were also located on the natural arteries of trade. During the summer months, caravans traveled over the high mountain roads with heavily laden wagons which were filled with merchandise for the great fairs and trade centers of Europe. Like the tourists of later centuries, the merchants required food and lodging for themselves and their workers, as well as care for their animals, relays of horses, and repairs for their wagons. Roads were narrow and steep, and the wear and tear on travelers and vehicles alike was great. Thus, a comfortable seasonal income was possible during the summer months. But in winter the roads were impassable, being buried deep in snow, and there was little to do. Since wood was abundant and easy to obtain, carving became an engaging occupation for all ages.

In some of the toy-making villages, the development of wooden toys had its beginning in the production of such simple household articles as wooden spoons, kitchen utensils, boxes of various kinds, and other useful articles. Then, the country folk began to make dolls, little wagons similar to those they saw on the roads, and animals, both domestic and wild, which were familiar to them. In

55

The toymaker plies his trade.

later years, as a world market for all kinds of wooden toys developed, their descendants often carved many exotic beasts for Noah's arks, beasts which they had never actually seen. The merchants, traveling the highroads in summer, were attracted to these toys, and bought them to take home to their own children. With this encouragement, the peasants began to make them in quantity. Putting them in wooden knapsacks which were strapped to their backs, they traveled about the surrounding countryside, peddling them. However, as the demand for the toys increased, there was little time for selling, since production in quantity was needed.

Agents, or middlemen, then began to take the local products and find markets for them in the great trade centers of Europe. Even though Nuremberg became the headquarters for distribution and, to a great extent, developed control of the industry, there were enterprising agents who left their native toy-making villages to represent their neighbors in the trade centers. In later years, some of them returned to build substantial homes in the villages of their birth. The demand for these beautifully carved toys increased, and a thriving business developed.

As the industry became centralized in Nuremberg, some of the originality expressed by the early carvers was lost. Patterns, in certain types of toys which proved popular in various parts of the world, became more or less stylized. Gradually, the demand for particular types made it necessary to place orders for the production of large quantities in all the toy-making villages, based on specific patterns. Soon it was not easy to trace the source of any particular toy, since it did not matter much where it was made, or by whom. Obviously, demands of the world market set in motion a certain amount of standardization, and the Nuremberg agents were anxious to please their customers in France, Russia, Great Britain, the Netherlands, and the United States. As long as hand skills were used, the toys never gave the feeling or appearance of being mass-produced. Ideas were swapped without much thought of origin. Later, the advent of machinery was, to a large extent, a limiting factor as far as originality in craftsmanship was concerned, but these toys were noted for their sturdy construction, their beauty of design, their bright colors, and their over-all eye appeal. What was more important, children everywhere loved them.

It was at Oberammergau, the home of the famed Passion Play, that the first wooden toys were made in quantity. Understandably enough, it was the outgrowth of the talent used in carving religious and devotional objects such as crucifixes, figures of the Holy Family and the saints. This home industry, begun in the late 1500's, showed remarkable advance in the years following the Thirty Years' War. In 1681, the carvers organized "a carver's guild, not a craftsman's union, as was usual elsewhere, for the men of Oberammergau felt themselves to be true artists." This distinction, made by Karl Gröber, noted German toy historian, emphasizes the true artistry of these early toys which were made in quantities and shipped to various parts of the world. Since these highly skilled carvers had their own agents in the leading cities of Europe, their work became widely known and was in great demand. This community was famous for "tubbing" wooden toys — that is, painting them, and carvers in various parts of Germany sent their products to Oberammergau to be finished.

The Lange family, whose name has been widely known to every well informed

A toy village similar to one cherished by Queen Victoria as a child.

Essex Institute Collection

traveler for generations, achieved a notable reputation in the toy field even before Nuremberg became famous as the toy depot of Germany. Today, thousands of visitors who travel to this famed community delight in the great collection, housed in the village Museum, which includes movable fortresses complete with soldiers, trumpets and drummers, hobbyhorses, toy animals, wagons, and all the other favorite toys of the period. There is also a notable collection of wooden soldiers of various wars, whose colorful uniforms make history come alive in a museum case. This renowned community is credited as being the birthplace of Noah's ark.

Berchtesgaden, also, made an early start in the home toy industry, and became known for sawmills, dolls, organ grinders, mouse cages, coaches, wagons, slaughtermen and blacksmiths, nutcrackers, pea shooters, Easter toys, religious figures, and many others. Several revolving toys of unusual interest were made here. Toys made in Berchtesgaden became so popular in the eighteenth century that the university students at Munich and Freising used to organize sledding parties in fancy dress costumes depicting the toys. Present-day department stores use this idea with automation to attract shoppers to their windows at Christmas.

In the Gröden Valley in South Tyrol, another toy center developed, and from it came more than three hundred skilled carvers, each specializing in one or several objects. At first, they turned to Oberammergau for painting, or tubbing, until they had acquired sufficient skill. This remote valley, referred to as the Toy Valley, had agents in more than one hundred cities on the Continent, and yet the population of the area included only thirty-five hundred people.

As the industry grew and higher tariffs were imposed, the home toy industry was affected seriously, and the making of toys in these great centers dwindled. A substitute for wood, made of dough and lime which was pressed into molds, gave an opportunity for making cheaper toys. The process, referred to as *drücken,* or squeezing, made for greater production, but the toys were not durable enough to stand the handling involved in shipping. Then the toy makers turned to papier-mâché, a mixture of paper pulp and cement, which proved most satisfactory for producing dolls' heads in great quantity.

58

At Erzgebirge in Saxony, toy-making replaced the mining industry in the eighteenth century. Interestingly enough, the playthings made here were distinctly primitive in their appearance, by design. They were made to suggest what they were meant to be, in order to stimulate the imagination of children. Typical was a group of animals for a Noah's ark or farmyard, arranged on a twisted ring which could be removed easily for play. These became objects of barter among the natives of Africa, and were equally popular in the Indies and in America. Despite economic changes and mechanization, the making of toys in this area has remained a home industry, reflecting the individuality and creative ability of the carvers of the Erzgebirge.

Glass toys were made at Lauscha in Thüringia, in the forests of Bavaria, and in Bohemia and Passau. Lauscha became widely known for the production of Christmas-tree ornaments as well. American merchants who visited this community in central Germany used to marvel at the skill of the glass blowers. They often worked under primitive conditions, using glass tubing and a single Bunsen burner to produce heat enough to fashion objects of various kinds. Clay toys

Jack-in-the-Box made in Germany, circa 1880–1900.

Courtesy, 1956 Manual of Doll Collectors of America.
Collections of Mrs. Earl Andrews and Mrs. Richard Merrill

59

Toymakers at work.

also were popular, and being easy to produce, were made in quantity by country potters all over Germany. Much of the pottery was used to equip the famous Nuremberg kitchens, or to fashion whistles in the form of animals. Curiously enough, the shapes of these whistles do not vary greatly from those made in other countries or from the models of antiquity. As Karl Gröber has pointed out, "They remain ever the same since they are made for the needs of one who has never yet changed in what he demands from playthings, namely the child."

At the beginning of the twentieth century, toy manufacturing was one of Germany's most important industries, and one-fourth of all the toys produced there were shipped to the United States. Flexible tariffs made possible the importing of enormous quantities from Sonneberg and other toy centers to meet the demands of the mass market. Sonneberg, in the Thuringian Mountains, was only a few hours by train from Berlin and had a population of about fifteen thousand persons at the time. Nearly half of all the playthings produced in this particular community found their way to America. Much of the production was carried on in the heart of the town, in ancient houses located on narrow streets stretching out from the market place toward the slopes of the nearby mountains.

As elsewhere in Germany, entire families, sometimes as many as four generations, were engaged in production under the same roof. All day long and well into the evening, they labored, sewing doll bodies, making dolls' dresses, carving and painting animals and other kinds of wooden toys. Gathered about the kitchen table — grandma in her cap, father with his leather apron, and all the rest of the family in their places — the toy makers used their nimble fingers

60

with the precise skill of automatons. A family of five who specialized in tiny lambs turned out 250 to 300 dozen each week. While many of the toys were standard items, produced year after year, new methods and techniques, as well as new ideas, were being introduced constantly. The Teddy bear craze, the fad for Caruso monkeys, the ever-changing trends of fashion in the doll world — all were familiar topics of conversation with these unsophisticated folk whose whole life was circumscribed by the limits of the busy toy-making town where they lived. What would American children want next?

Most of the operations were performed at home, except for certain kinds of sewing, cutting, and stamping, which were done in the town factories where the working day ranged from ten to thirteen hours. Wages were unbelievably low, and entire families earned but a few dollars a week. For the most part, decorating was a hand process which gave even the cheap toys a certain individuality and charm. On the other hand, toy making in Nuremberg had become almost entirely a factory operation.

Every Saturday, it was a common sight to see the women of neighboring towns and villages arrive in Sonneberg by train. The week's production was taken either to the factory, which supplied them with raw materials, or to the warehouse of an export merchant. Both young and old arrived at the depot, carrying enormous baskets on their backs. These baskets were usually three feet high and of equal diameter. When the load was not too heavy, a long, flat basket, three by five feet, was bound to the top of the first basket and piled so high that it projected several feet above the head of the carrier. These loads, which frequently weighed a hundred pounds or more, were kept securely in position by the use of stout shoulder straps. Those who lived on the outskirts of Sonneberg made their way on foot, often carrying their bulky products over steep inclines and rough roads. Such was the life of the toy maker.

The selling of wooden toys to the world was accomplished by colorful sample books and catalogs or "magazines," as they were called by the manufacturers. These dreambooks, for such they were, showed pictures of scores of toys. The "pedagogical magazine" of Georg Hieronymus Bestelmeier, the earliest of them all, listed no less than twelve hundred different toys.

CHAPTER 9

Let's Play Soldiers

Despite the advances of the atomic age, the lure of the tin toy soldier has never faded completely, even in our own day. Yet, trends in toys have changed considerably since Robert Louis Stevenson wrote the following, from *The Land of Counterpane:*

> And sometimes for an hour or so
> I watched my leaden soldiers go,
> With different uniforms and drills
> Among the bedclothes, through the hills.

Whatever the reactions of the average youngster who looks at those long rows of lead figures, sometimes seen in museums and often found in private collections, they have a curious appeal for grownups who collect them avidly. And not all of these collectors are actively or remotely associated with military affairs. Then too, toy soldiers are being made again in quantity and sold in gift shops and even in "five and tens," as they used to be, but a plastic substance has been substituted for the metal of earlier days.

The story of the tin soldier is steeped in history and romance, much of which has been forgotten. It all began with the exploits of Frederick the Great, King of Prussia from 1740 to 1786, which captured the imagination of the whole world. His victories and his skill in the strategy of war were so popular a topic of discussion that the introduction of tin soldiers, made in Nuremberg from 1760 on, resulted in a craze for these toys that reached to the far corners of the earth. If any toy may be said to mirror an episode of history, and a highly dramatic one at that, surely the tin soldier has few peers.

Tin soldiers, often referred to as the "dolls of boyhood," were never exclusively the province of boys; but, on the whole, they had little appeal for girls until the time of the Napoleonic wars. Even then, they never replaced dolls in the girls' world. On the other hand, dolls have never been exclusively the property of girls, but they have always held stronger appeal for them than for boys. Curiously enough, only about 10 per cent of all the dolls made are boy dolls.

Toy horses and warriors were a part of boyhood even before the time of the famous Trojan horse. Tiny replicas of this extraordinary horse which have been found are believed to have been either toys or souvenirs of the historic event at Ilium. It was the custom in ancient times to visit historic sites, and there were

62

souvenir sellers even then. Excavations made at Smyrna in Greece during the past century revealed a tiny metal carriage with a pair of horses. A miniature soldier in bronze, of Roman origin, and figures of armoured knights in tin, dating from the Middle Ages, have been described as other ancestors of the tin soldier. However, they were individual pieces rather than parts of large sets like the tin soldiers produced in quantity in the eighteenth century. A drawing from a twelfth-century manuscript shows two boys playing at a table with two knights whose fighting ability was manipulated by strings attached to movable parts. Knights made of clay or glazed stoneware provided amusement for German boys in the fifteenth and sixteenth centuries. In 1516, Maximilian I, Emperor of the Holy Roman Empire, who was often referred to as "the last of the knights," had a picture drawn of his childhood to illustrate his biography. This woodcut, fascinating in its detail, shows a group of adults and children at play. Of special interest are the mounted knights in armor astride horses on wheels. The game was called playing at "tilting," and the object was the dexterous use of the lance, manipulated by hand or by cords in such a way that one knight would unseat the other. It is said that the Emperor delighted in this toy, even in his declining years, and ordered a skilled helmet-maker to fashion two similar knights as a gift for King Ludwig II of Hungary.

During the seventeenth and eighteenth centuries, members of the French court, both young and old, had a keen interest in toys, especially those made of precious metals, and automatons as well! In fact, rulers of many countries and their families indulged their whims in unusual toys of all kinds. As a child, Louis XIII played with lead soldiers, which he placed in holes cut in a board. In 1650, he commissioned the making of an army of soldiers cast in silver for his twelve-year-old son, Louis XIV. They were designed by a famous French artist and created by the goldsmith Merlin at a cost of 50,000 thalers (about $35,000). Perhaps the most fabulous set of soldiers ever made were those produced in Nuremberg in 1672 at the request of Louis XIV for his son. The celebrated war minister, Sébastien de Vauban, was sent to the great toy center to supervise its production. Each of the three-and-a-half-inch figures was equipped with an automatic device by a noted compass-maker of the day. This great collection was later described by the German historian Weigel, who recalled from memory that the soldiers "went through the usual war manoeuvres very ably; they marched to the left and to right, doubled their ranks, lowered their weapons, struck fire, shot off, and retreated. Then the lancemen tried to knock the cavalrymen out of their saddles, but these were quite prepared to defend themselves by firing their pistols."

In those days, it was a practice of goldsmiths to model figures in tin to guide them in fashioning subjects in the more precious metals. Then, too, there was a vogue for pendants which were worn on guard chains. These were figures of tin in the form of soldiers, knights, and favorite saints which might have been mistaken easily for toys. Small animals of tin were made by trinket casters in Nuremberg in 1578.

However, such marvels were not for every boy, since they were costly beyond compare. The creation of the tin soldier as an inexpensive toy was the accomplishment of Andreas Hilpert, a master craftsman in tin and pewter, who began to cast tin figures in Nuremberg. He had obtained the freedom of the city and

63

of his guild to launch his venture. At first, the little flat figures were made so that they could be placed in stands, and not all of them were soldiers by any means. It was Hilpert's custom to sign his work, either with his initials or his full name. Animals both familiar and exotic were modeled from engravings and arranged under their correct zoological classifications with their Latin names inscribed. Deer, moose, reindeer, elk, and others including monkeys, which were very popular, could be had either plain or colored. As Karl Gröber points out in *Children's Toys of Bygone Days,* "The social life, too, of the period was not overlooked by the Hilperts, and we have rococo gardens with cleverly cut hedges and fountains, with gardeners at work and vine-dressers picking grapes, with promenading ladies and their gallants, and, what was so popular at the end of the eighteenth century, a sledge party . . . figures of gods and goddesses, and groups symbolizing the four seasons and the four elements. Again, we find gipsy encampments and herdsmen with their cows at pasture; while many single figures, such as a man in a dark mantle or a red coat, almost leave the impression that the heroes of the stage of the day must have served as models for them."

However, tin soldiers were produced in great numbers because they were easy to produce and paint in quantity. This method of handling also made possible the lowering of prices, so that a large market was created. To meet the demands of other nations, soldiers dressed in uniforms of many countries were soon being turned out in Nuremberg. To quote Gröber, "Little warriors from all over the globe, packed in the neat little boxes supplied by the small handworkers of Berchtesgaden, were to be bought in every toy shop." It was not long before soldiers of nearly every war in recent times were to be produced, as the years passed.

The Hilpert family lost its monopoly in the manufacture of tin toys as other tin founders in Nuremberg and elsewhere pursued this lucrative business. Obviously, the world was larger than the Nuremberg tinsmiths realized, because the production of tin soldiers and other tin toys spread to all parts of Germany by the early part of the nineteenth century.

Swiss craftsmen also turned their talents to the tin toy business, but Germany had developed production to such a high degree that it held a virtual monopoly. In the late 1860's, hollow soldiers, in contrast to those of solid metal, were made in England, and these became immensely popular in Great Britain. It was an attempt to break the German monopoly in the making of this popular toy that spurred the British on, but the Germans and the Japanese soon began to copy the English product. However, the English manufacturers continued to make tin soldiers in great numbers. In 1936, a set of eighty-three pieces, called "The Changing of the Guard," was offered for sale, complete with an elegant coach in which King Edward VIII was seated comfortably. News of King Edward VIII's abdication not only stirred the world, it sent the toy makers in a scurry to fashion new occupants for the coach, in the persons of George VI and his Queen.

Axel Munthe, in *Memories and Vagaries,* recalls an incident after the War of 1870 that gives us an interesting sidelight on the production of tin soldiers in France. The import duty on these figures made in Germany was but a trifle, and France was flooded with them until "a poor workman at Belleville got a sudden inspiration, an inspiration that, since then, has engendered an army which would realize the dream of eternal peace and keep in check the assembled troops of all

Europe, were it a question of numbers alone. He sets on foot 5,000,000 soldiers a year. The origin of these soldiers is humble, but so was Napoleon's. They spring from old sardine boxes. . . .The warriors are cut out from the bottom of the box. The lids and sides are used for making guns, railway carriages, ambulances. . . . All this may seem very unimportant to you at first sight, but in Belleville a large manufactory has been founded on this idea of utilising old sardine boxes, which occupies no less than two hundred workmen and produces every year over two milliards (billions) of tin toys. . . . After retreating for years, the French tin soldiers once more advance; the German spiked-helmets retire every Christmas from the conquered positions in French nurseries, and maybe the time is not far off when the tricolor will wave over the toy shops of Berlin — a small revenge in awaiting the great one."

The establishment of the Nuremberg scale, which determined that the figure of a grown man was not to be more than one-and-one-third inches, with all other figures conforming to this scale, was a prime factor to the booming German trade. Thus, games could be played by youngsters, and war maneuvers planned by military men on an equal basis, without engaging in a battle between giants and dwarfs.

The method of production changed but little over the years. Forms for both sides of the figures were cut from slate and engraved, after which they were carefully imposed one on the other, and the cavity filled with melted tin. For the most part, painting was done by home workers. Because of the great demand for all types of figures and the skill with which they were produced, the industry in some measure replaced the production of wooden toys in Germany during the nineteenth century.

The tin soldier had come a long way from those miniatures of baked clay, wood, and metal which had amused the children of the Ancients. In contrast to the highly standardized workmanship of German craftsmen, there were soldiers made in France with parts molded separately and soldered together. Wooden soldiers made in Thuringia and other regions of Germany were sometimes referred to as "Biffins" in the heydey of penny toys in Victorian England. Toy makers in Czechoslovakia, Russia, Denmark, Sweden, and other countries also produced various types and kinds of wooden soldiers.

Other materials included a combination of wood and flour paste, rubber, gum tragacanth or tragant, as it was called, mixed with sugar and meal, and even chocolate were used. Cardboard and paper soldiers came to be popular in both Europe and America during the nineteenth century. During the time of Napoleon, a German baker cut five thousand figures out of paper and painted them with great skill, so that all of Napoleon's regiments were easily identifiable. Ninepins shaped like French soldiers, commonly referred to as "skittles" in England, became a vogue there in the 1870's.

For centuries, boys and girls alike have enjoyed playing at war, in every generation. Guns, cannon, swords, drums, trumpets, uniforms complete with trappings, assorted headgear, and the like have provided excitement, amusement, and an occasional accident on a dull day when it was not fit to play outside. The spirit of play among adults has been from the collector's angle, and the tin soldier offered variety enough to keep even the most avid collector happy in bygone days, as it does today.

66

Overland cast-iron circus band wagon of the 1890--1910 period, made
by the Kenton Hardware Company of Kenton, Ohio.

Collection of Richard Merrill

Mechanical tin toys of familiar comic characters of the 1920 era, made
in Germany.

Collection of Richard Merrill

Chapter **10**

Toys That Taste Good

Toys go hand in hand with good things to eat, and, for centuries, cookies, cakes, and candy in the form of toys have delighted grownups and children alike. Edible dolls are as old as the toy doll. In German culture, dolls or figures made from dough were called "picture bread." In fact, figures in the form of domestic animals can be traced back to antiquity, when they were used as substitutes for animals offered for sacrifice in religious ceremonies. Among the Egyptians and the ancient Greeks, human figures made of dough were associated with family festivals. Like many pagan customs, the practice of making them was continued long after the advent of Christianity, even though the original purposes for which they were made were forbidden. Among the Norwegians, in the thirteenth century, a law was enacted prohibiting the baking of dough in human form, and this was strictly enforced.

During the Middle Ages, dolls of bread cut in the forms of saints were made for the children on the feast days of favorite saints. In *Dolls and Puppets,* Max von Boehn observed, "The gingerbread doll had a tenacious life, perhaps because it appealed to the stomach and not to the spirit. The shapes which it assumed remained the same for centuries." There was an old tradition in Germany concerning three holy virgins, St. Einbede, St. Warbede and St. Willebede of the early church, but their names do not appear in contemporary directories of the saints. In the Middle Ages, they were commemorated in gingerbread figures and the patterns are still used in Germany. Freshly baked gingerbread in any form can always be delectable, but cut in the form of a man or an animal and decorated with currants, raisins, or some kind of sugar frosting, it is and always has been all the more appealing.

So popular was gingerbread in England that there were fairs where only gingerbread and toys were sold. Each year in Birmingham, two gingerbread fairs were held until well into the nineteenth century, and, as Mrs. E. Nevill Jackson reminds us in *Toys of Other Days,* the warrant for holding the fairs was given back in the thirteenth century. Long lines of market stalls, filled with gingerbread in every imaginable shape and form, were interspersed with booths filled with toys.

Gingerbread men were called "husbands" at the English fairs, and were often referred to as "Jim Crows" in nineteenth century America. Nathaniel Hawthorne mentions them as favorites in Hepzibah Pyncheon's cent shop in his *House of Seven Gables,* along with elephants made of gingerbread. In Europe it was customary to decorate this spicy toy-cake with gold — or Dutch-leaf. When broken, or when the gilt peeled off, they were sold at half price, from which comes the old expression, "to take the gilt off the gingerbread." Also, the expression "gingerbread" has been frequently associated with the geegaws and jigsaw cut-outs so common in Victorian architecture and with furnishings which, today, are considered overly ornate.

In Europe, it used to be a custom of shopkeepers to give gingerbread men, various kinds of cookies and candies, often with the shop name stamped on them, to children, either to pacify them when they came to the shop with their mothers, or as a friendly gesture, or as good-will advertising. This old-time custom found its way to America at an early date.

Gingerbread hornbooks and battledore books were popular in eighteenth-century England. A famous London street cry, offering book gingerbread with the alphabet in it at a half-penny a slice, was commonplace for more than a century and a half, and lasted well into the nineteenth century. William Hogarth immortalized the gingerbread man when he introduced him into his picture *The Idle Apprentice Executed at Tyburn.* There had been many a gingerbread seller, but this man named Ford, who was a colorful figure everywhere in London and at Bartholomew Fair as well, was known as "Tiddy Doll the gingerbread baker," and Hogarth placed him in his own Hall of Fame. Tiddy Doll disappeared from his usual place in the Haymarket in 1752, for he had gone on a junket to the country fairs. A Grub Street newshawk wrote a fanciful half-penny account of his murder, and it sold as fast as the gingerbread which Tiddy Doll peddled.

In fact, as Charles Hindley describes him in *A History of the Cries of London,* he was "hailed as the king of itinerant tradesmen. He was a constant attendant in the crowd at all metropolitan fairs, mob meetings, Lord Mayor's shows, public executions, and all other holiday and festive gatherings! In his person he was tall, well made, and his features handsome. He affected to dress like a person of rank; white and gold lace suit of clothes, lace ruffled shirt, laced hat and feather, white stockings, with the addition of a white apron. Among his harangues to gain customers, take the following piece as a fair sample of the whole:—

"Mary, Mary, where are you *now,* Mary? I live, when at home, at the second house in Little diddy-ball-street, two steps under ground, with a wiscum, riscum, and a why-not. Walk in, ladies and gentlemen; my shop is on the second floor backwards, with a brass knocker on the door, and steel steps before it. Here is your nice gingerbread, it will melt in your mouth like a red-hot brickbat, and rumble in your insides like Punch and his wheelbarrow." He always finished his address by singing this tag end of some popular ballad:—

> Ti-tid-ty, ti-tid-ty. Ti-tid-ty — tiddy loll.
> Ti-tid-ty, ti-tid-ty. Ti-tid-ty — tiddy doll.

Ships, watches, flint-lock guns, grandfather's clocks, the King on horseback, roosters, rabbits, fair ladies dressed in the style of Queen Anne, and numerous other subjects were among the cutouts made from gingerbread. The devil and St. Nicholas hardly seem like suitable companions, but figures of the devil made from gingerbread, chocolate, baked fruit, or raisins are still to be found in German shops prior to December 6, Nicholas's feast day. They were also sold at a fair held in Vienna on his feast day, and some of the figures were life-size.

Makers and sellers of gingerbread have left their mark on the American scene as well. In *The American Notebooks,* Hawthorne told of the gingerbread men

Tiddy Doll, the gingerbread baker.

he saw at country fairs and of the booths set up on Boston Common for the Fourth of July, 1838, "selling gingerbread, sugar plums, and confectionery." In the days when hawkers roamed America, selling all manner of articles at fairs or from door to door, gingerbread sellers offered their wares with the same friendly spirit as today's popcorn and ice cream vendors.

Although the gingerbread man has disappeared, the fun of making cookies in the form of toys has by no means been forgotten or neglected. At Christmas, and often for birthdays and special holidays, these fancy cookies appear in bakeries,

70

at church fairs, and in homes where the age-old art of cookery is still a family tradition. Louise LaGorce of Washington, D. C., carried on her hobby with toy cookies to such an extent that she wrote a most unusual and practical book called *The Christmas Cookie Tree.* In it she tells how she uses white dough and brown dough to make all manner of figures, decorated with fancy icing and little ornaments. Turkeys and clowns, boys and girls, rabbits, raccoons, angels, pigs, dogs, lambs, elephants, zebras, monkeys, and a host of other creatures, together with castles and cottages, have become a tradition with Mrs. LaGorce, and her simple, easy-to-follow instructions have opened the way to a new adventure for many a housewife.

As these paragraphs are written, I am aware that there are many other amusing and delightful forms of edible toys which are not mentioned here. To write about all of them fully would be to attempt a tidy little book devoted to toys for good eating.

As Lesley Gordon reminds us in *Peepshow into Paradise,* the famous pig of "Tom, Tom, the Piper's Son" was not a live pig, for Tom would have had to eat it raw. It was a sugar pig that piemen used to sell in the streets in the eighteenth century.

Easter is a special time of year for enjoying sweets, particularly among those who have abstained during the days of Lent. For a century and a half, the egg, the chicken, and the rabbit have been used as molds for chocolate and various mixtures of sugar. The imagination of confectioners and housewives has often been challenged to provide new delights for young folks. They are much tastier than the handsomest colored egg, and it is easier to eat more of them.

A special kind of Easter cake, made in the form of a rabbit, using raisins for eyes and a colored egg protruding beneath the rabbit's tail, has been popular among the Pennsylvania Dutch for several generations. Local bakers used to make them in quantity, using the same dough they prepared for bread, and sometimes these cakes were made at home at Eastertime. The custom is still observed in the "Dutch" country, as it is in Germany, where it has been treasured for centuries.

Those gaily colored and elaborately decorated eggs, which are an important part of the Easter observance in various parts of Europe, often fall into the category of keepsakes rather than toys. The ornately decorated shells are much too handsome to break, and there are always plenty of ordinary colored eggs available to eat.

Among the Poles and Ukrainians, the art of decorating eggs involves unusual skill and imagination. Melted beeswax is applied before dyeing, and the process repeated as the eggs are dipped in various colors. These "designed" eggs were known as *pysanki,* and each is original in its design. They were blessed by the parish priest before they were presented to friends, and many were kept as cherished heirlooms. Symbols like the sun for good fortune, the rooster for fulfillment of wishes, the stag or deer for good health, and flowers for love conveyed the intended message.

The Easter-egg tree, in many ways the counterpart of the Christmas tree, has become a new tradition in America in the past ten years, because of the widespread popularity of a delightful children's book, *The Egg Tree,* by Katherine

Milhous. This custom of decorating evergreens or leafless trees with colored eggs, a novelty among the Pennsylvania Dutch, had its origin in the years following the Civil War. The older practice of suspending or impaling eggs in their natural colors on bushes and small trees outdoors was a custom of earlier date. Of German origin, this fashion was vividly portrayed in the color lithographs circulated in this country before the turn of the century. It was also practiced in other northern European countries.

Another curious form of egg decoration, formerly seen in Pennsylvania Dutch homes, was the Easter-egg bird. This was a decorated shell in which four holes were made, one for the head, two for the wings and one for the tail, plus an opening for attaching the bird to a thread so it could be hung. These birds were popular a century ago and lasted indefinitely, if not roughly handled.

Another sport, popular in Europe and America, is rolling hard-boiled eggs against each other or down hill. The child who retains the last uncracked egg is the winner. This pleasant pastime, believed to have been observed annually at Easter on the lawn of the White House in Washington since the presidency of James Madison, has been the subject of many fascinating stories.

In Spain, a pastry that was originally designed to resemble a Paschal lamb often turns out to look more like a monkey at the hands of amateur cooks. Thus, it is referred to as the "Easter she-monkey" and is decorated lavishly with almonds, candied fruits, and eggs. The colors of the eggs used are symbols.

Lesley Gordon, in *A Pageant of Dolls,* recalls that "Yorkshire used to have a bread doll of its own, made as nearly as possible to look like a real baby, with fingers and toes marked on it and a small dab of dough for a nose; this doughy infant was lightly baked and dressed in real white babyclothes."

Nineteenth-century dining-room cupboards and cent shops provided many delights, as recorded by Alice Morse Earle in 1893. She wrote, "few comfit-makers made 'Lemon Pil Candy, Angelica Candy, Candy'd Eryngo Root & Carroway Comfits;' and a few sweetmeats came to port in foreign vessels, 'Sugar'd Corrinder Seeds,' 'Glaz'd Almonds,' and strings of rock-candy. Whole jars of the latter adamantine, crystalline, saccharine delight graced the shelves of many a colonial cupboard. And I suppose favored Salem children, the happy sons and daughters of opulent epicurean Salem shipowners, had even in colonial days Black Jacks and Salem Gibraltars. The first-named dainties, though dearly loved by Salem lads and lasses, always bore — indeed, do still bear — too strong a flavor of liquorice." She also recalled that "the good ship Ann and Hope brought into Providence one hundred years ago, as part of her cargo, eight boxes of sweetmeats and twenty tubs of sugar candy, and on the succeeding voyage sternly fetched no sweets, but brought instead forty-eight boxes of rhubarb."

Cookies as Christmas toys, and many of the recipes for making them, came to America from Germany more than two hundred years ago. In the Dutch country of Pennsylvania, where many old traditions have been cherished and kept alive, "Matzabaums, moshey and belly-guts" were favorite confections for Christmas a century and a half ago. Matzabaum is "a wonderful good" cookie or cake, while the other two items belong definitely to the realm of candy, but are tasty. The name "matzabaum" is derived from the German marzipan — or marchpane, a candy made of pounded almonds. In the Dutch country the "pan" was dropped

and "baum," or tree, added, because this fancy bit was widely used to decorate the Christmas tree. Marzipan, in a variety of fruit forms, is a sweet toy steeped in the traditions of many parts of the Old World.

These cookies were cut from clay, wooden, or tin molds made in the shape of butterflies, birds, fish, animals, and "such-like." Rolling pins, with a variety of patterns cut in the roller, were also used. The dough was rich in sugar, eggs, spices, and finely chopped nuts, and produced delicious cookies which were usu-

ally baked, but some kinds were simply set out to dry on the pantry shelf, since they did not require baking because of their heavy consistency. Those made of starch and elaborately decorated were primarily for the trees. Simon Snyder Rathvon, writing in the Lancaster *Weekly Intelligencer* December 28, 1881, was recording his memoirs of earlier days when he wrote: "They were made of white dough, and at least two kinds: one containing sweetening and the other none . . . They were embellished with animals, trees, birds, flowers, bushes, men, women, and children, pressed in a sort of 'bold relief' upon the one side, and they were gaudily painted with red, yellow, green, blue, etc., and when the youngsters commenced sucking them, for the small quantity of sugar they contained, their hands

73

and their faces from their mouths to their eyes presented a ludicrous aspect of commingled daubery."

A brown dough that, when baked, looks like a pretzel (without the salt crystals) is still used in Czechoslovakia to make some of the most fanciful Christmas cookies imaginable. They are made from molds shaped in the forms of people, animals, birds, and flowers, and executed with all the detail found in sculpture. In fact, they are so intriguing and fascinating to look at, that one would hardly think of eating them. They require infinite patience and skill in the making, and are the remnants of a confectionery art which became popular in the nineteenth century in Europe and America.

Toy soldiers made of sugar were all the vogue in the days following the Civil War. A paste, made of sugar meal and a binder like gum tragacanth, an aromatic gum derived from an Asiatic shrub, was prepared and poured into molds. The figures were gaily painted, which made them not too tasty, but for the Christmas tree they were superb ornaments.

Until the eighteenth century, when porcelain was used, delicately fashioned figurines made of a sugar composition or marzipan were popular for table ornaments at court banquets. The making of these was considered a highly skilled art, and confectioners rivalled one another in creating original pieces, even some that moved. They made up sample pieces for display in their shop windows. The fancy cakes and wedding cake ornaments seen in bakeries today are all that remain of this art.

A soldered tin and wood toy engine, manufactured by Hull and
Stafford Company, Clinton, Connecticut, 1860–1880.

Collection of Richard Merrill

Tin buggy and horse, about 1874.

Essex Institute Toy Collection

CHAPTER II

The Magic of Music and Sound

Mention of musical and sound toys brings to mind many pleasant hours spent with music boxes, percussion instruments, carousels, and a host of others, from the rattle to the bull roarer. Not to be overlooked either are the various kinds of bell toys that made nursery days a blend of joy and confusion, with not a few headaches, as they still do. But, of all the truly musical toys of childhood, none was more greatly enjoyed by all ages than the hand organ or "monkey" organ. The organ grinder with his monkey was a blend of musician and clown, and something of a philosopher too, as he moved down the street playing old-time tunes. Alfred Noyes recalled with nostalgia some of those unforgettable moments of his English boyhood when he wrote this verse in *The Barrel Organ*.

> Verdi, Verdi, when you wrote Il Trovatore, did you dream
>   Of the City when the sun sinks low,
> Of the organ and the monkey and the many-colored stream
> On the Piccadilly pavement, of the myriad eyes that seem
> To be litten for a moment with a wild Italian gleam
> As *A che la morte* parodies the world's eternal theme
>   And pulses with the sunset glow?

If the crowd did not gather soon enough, he was always quick to change his tune. If his music seemed a bit dull at times, his friendly monkey, usually with a long rope or chain attached to his waist, made up for it with his antics. Here, indeed, was a glimpse of nostalgia and charm from street scenes of the Old World, and fair days, too. In the heyday of these performers, most of the hand-organ men came from Italy. Until a few decades ago, all types and kinds of hand organs and hurdy-gurdys were to be seen on city streets, but they have disappeared. The organ grinder used to be as punctual as the first crocus in spring. He made the summer days pleasant and gay for young and old, for he was always on hand for parades and fairs, and whenever the circus came to town. As autumn came, he was still a familiar figure as we traveled to and from school. Only winter sent him into hibernation, since cold weather was not to the liking of the monkey. Actually, monkeys are known to be extremely sensitive to cold, and the commonest cause of death among them is one due to exposure. It took considerable time to train a monkey, and since he was so important to the success of the operation,

owners took the best of care of the "little fellow." Actually, during the winter months organ grinders plied their trade from Charleston south, and some even traveled to the orange groves of California. In the 1920's, licenses for monkeys were outlawed in New York City, for these nimble and lovable creatures had a habit of stealing things from apartments which they sometimes entered as they scrambled up the sides of buildings. They also had a way of biting children who became too friendly or tormented them.

The circus as we used to know it has vanished. So, too, have the old-time parades, which were often miles long and took hours to pass a given point. Even the fairs and carnivals have changed in this mechanical age. The organ grinder, like so many of the peddlers and vendors of goodies and toys, has passed down the same road.

With his music and his monkey, whose bag of tricks was ever the same, the organ grinder, nevertheless, provided more fun than the best wind-up toy ever made. And to watch them both cost only a penny or two, tossed to the monkey. Robert Cortes Holliday recalled these memories vividly when he described a monkey known as Jocko in his book of essays *In the Neighborhood of Murray Hill.* "What a delicious star comedian he was when, in the days of yesteryear, whole neighborhoods came out to relish seeing him, in his gorgeous ruffled and be-frogged jacket, receive with a flamboyant bow the pennies in his pointed velvet hat! And when he would shin up the side of a house to welcomers at upper windows, what a hilarious cheer!" The costumes which these little comedians wore were usually made by the organ grinder or his wife, and both the colors used and the style of tailoring expressed the whim of the grinder.

The name hurdy-gurdy was commonly used in reference to various kinds of instruments that used to be played on the streets, such as the barrel organ, grinder organ, street organ, hand organ, and monkey organ. Actually, the hurdy-gurdy, which originated in France in Medieval times, was a drone instrument with hammer strings which were set in vibration by the friction of a wheel. The sound-chest, or box, was either rectangular or shaped like a guitar. Within it was a leather-covered wheel, coated with rosin, which was operated by a crank. The mechanism, adapted in various ways, paved the way for a variety of musical curiosities.

The barrel organ, on the other hand, was a portable instrument, sometimes set on a wagon or mounted on wheels. Music was produced by a cylinder fixed with pins and staples. The opened valves admitted wind to pipes from a bellows, which functioned by means of the revolving cylinder. Because it was developed in the Netherlands, it was commonly referred to as a Dutch organ. Two centuries or more ago, it was often made in a more elaborate form and was used in churches and chapels for the rendition of hymns and chants. In fact, this instrument was a source of great fascination to many of the noted musicians of the day. Men like Handel complained that its performance was greater than anything they could do, since anyone who wished, without the slightest skill in music, could play as many as eight tunes by merely turning the handle and then change the tunes. A miniature-type organ, known as a bird organ, inspired Mozart to write an Andante for it.

The familiar monkey organ, with its tiny pipes and bellows, played such old

77

The organ grinder delighted all ages.

favorite tunes as *Santa Lucia, Good-by, Good Luck, God Bless You, Beautiful Ohio, Always Blowing Bubbles, Till We Meet Again, Bright Eyes,* and dozens of other popular melodies of the day. Tunes changed with the musical hits of the day, and the organ grinders saw to it that their music boxes poured out what people liked to hear. These melody boxes were mounted on a stick, and usually the grinder carried the box, attached with a strap to his back, as he walked. When he stopped to play, the self-same strap over his shoulder helped to balance the instrument as he stood before his enchanted audience.

When Nathaniel Hawthorne wrote *The House of Seven Gables* in 1851, organ grinders were something of a novelty in the seaport towns of New England. The organ which Hawthorne described was a sort of combination peep show and music box. It contained a panel encased in glass, in which a series of little paper figures moved as the Italian boy, with the broad-brimmed hat, turned the crank. "The cobbler wrought upon a shoe; the blacksmith hammered his iron; the soldier waved his glittering blade; the lady raised a tiny breeze with her fan; the jolly toper swigged lustily at his bottle; a scholar opened his book with eager thirst for

78

knowledge, and turned his head to and fro along the page; the milkmaid energetically drained her cow; and a miser counted gold into his strongbox, — all at the same turning of a crank. Yes; and, moved by the selfsame impulse, a lover saluted his mistress on her lips!"

The earliest form of mechanical music is believed to be the carillon, an arrangement of bells or tuned cymbals, which was developed in ancient China long before the Christian era. In the fifteenth century, there were turret clocks in English church towers, that played tunes on bells; but these musical clocks were more popular in the Latin countries, where they played folk songs on weekdays and sacred music on Sundays. It was in Switzerland that musical watches were first made and sold in 1780. Then came the heyday of the music box, which remained popular until the introduction of the phonograph or gramophone and the player piano.

For sheer musical entertainment, when the hurdy-gurdy man was not around, the music box was a prime source of the pleasantest kind of diversion. The works for these little music makers were contained in snuff and jewel boxes, in jugs and bottles, in the tops of walking sticks, in miniature houses and churches, in toy carousels, and in dozens of other forms. The period from 1810 to 1910 was the golden era of popularity for tobacco and snuff. Women as well as men used snuff, and fancy boxes in which it was kept were extremely fashionable. Thus, the development of the music box provided great delight to users of snuff. An amazing variety of music was available in these boxes, including operatic selections, patriotic songs, ballads, folk songs, waltzes and popular tunes of music and dance halls.

Toy music boxes were first made about 1835. The earlist types were round metal boxes, fancily painted. These played a single tune and were operated by a crank. As the market developed, the demand became so great that not only were many kinds of novelties made, but the mechanics of operation were improved as well. Unique features of a mechanical nature were developed, and soon there were birds that moved, girls that danced, clowns that performed, and beautifully gowned young women who presided at pianos and organs pouring out the most delightful music. A life-size canary was the chief delight of Marie Antoinette, made by a Paris craftsman.

In Germany, the master toy makers of the world began to produce whistling men, described by John E. T. Clark in his book, *Music Boxes*. "These were miniature models of men or boys in various costumes, and when the mechanism was started, the models would whistle a song tune and, at the same time, nod their heads. These models were called 'whistling men' and stood nine inches to a foot in height. A man leaning against a lamp-post would whistle *We won't go home till morning;* the lamp was lit from a torch battery. A man carrying a lantern would whistle *Show me the way to go home*. A model of Uncle Sam would, of course, whistle *Yankee Doodle*. In some of the more expensive models, there would be two men, both playing musical instruments, and two song tunes would be whistled, one after the other. As regards the single figures, there were models to represent Charlie Chaplin, a negro, a tramp, a boy scout, and a man with a clock under his arm. All the figures were hand-carved and coloured. They would whistle airs appropriate to the character they were supposed to represent."

The story of bells and the pleasure they have brought is a saga that starts with the cradle and ends with the grave. Strangely enough, tiny bells were found in the tombs where children were laid in the days of the Catacombs at Rome. They can still be seen in the museum in the Vatican at Rome. The Greeks and Romans followed this custom in Pagan times, for it was believed that the toys which had provided pleasure should accompany the departed children on their journey to heaven.

Bailey's midget piano is a rare collector's item from the past century. Each of the dolls is connected with a key and when the piano is played the dolls bounce, swing, and turn circles in a most astonishing manner.

The Rushford Collections

Despite its fascination as a toy, we are reminded that the bell on wheels did not become a popular toy until the nineteenth century. Then, bells were fastened to every conceivable kind of toy that could be pulled, pushed, or rocked. Even jump ropes had bells attached, and many a tiny child today has a special delight in slippers with bells on, right out of the nursery-rhyme books. Some grownups like the sound of them, too. Hoops, in the days of ancient Greece, had all the lure of the recent craze for the hula hoop, but, in addition, those early hoops had spokes in them with bits of metal attached, which made a clanking sound as they were rolled. Add to the hoop a bell and a clapper, as was done in the nineteenth

80

century, and another step in the evolution of an old toy was brought about — one best enjoyed when there was space aplenty in the great outdoors.

Finely made toys, produced by silversmiths especially for infants, often ornamented with beautifully wrought bells attached to an elaborately fashioned chain with large links, were referred to as "coral and bells." These, together with a whistle and a teething stick, made of coral, agate, rock crystal, ivory, mother-of-pearl, bone, and similar materials, made a most enchanting toy for the children of those who could afford such luxuries. However, not all of these were fashioned of costly materials.

The age-old belief that children who wore necklaces made of beads carved from peony wood would be protected from epilepsy may have been the basis for these elaborate necklace-like rattles. At any rate, the hard substances used for teething sticks were used to make "anodyne necklaces." Fabulous claims were made for them in advertisements, similar to those which appeared before patent medicine advertising was subjected to government scrutiny. "The *New York Gazette,* revived in the *Weekly Post Boy* for October 17, 1748, carried a notice of anodyne necklaces, imported from London, in which it was claimed that children on the brink of the grave, through trouble with their teeth, miraculously recovered after wearing the necklace for one night." This and other curious facts about rattles are included in a pamphlet entitled *American Baby Rattles* by Harry B. Weiss. Many of the seventeenth-century artists like Vandyke, Rembrandt, and Holbein depicted them in their portraits of children.

Many of the toys that make sound, or noise for that matter, hardly can be called musical toys. Yet, in grouping toys according to their prime function, they are sometimes so classified. Rattles and whistles are among the earliest toys of childhood, and also those of the greatest antiquity. Many variations of the rattle have been used over the centuries, from the gourd found in nature to the most elaborate types in silver, but its appeal for little tots has not changed. Rattles have long been associated with the working of magic among primitive tribes, and have been considered sacred objects, as well. The Eskimos used them to entice seals into the water. Crude clay objects, shaped like pears, pigs, or little barrels, are among the oldest that remain. Painted and decorated kinds made of wood, metal, rubber, bone, and other materials, often with ornate chains, bells, tassels, and ribbons attached, have been produced by the millions down through the years. The age of celluloid, which began with a patent for a rattle granted in 1869, and the use of plastics in our own day, have added an innovation in design and appearance. A collection of rattles, dating from the earliest times to the present, shows more than fancy in the whims of man and the uses to which they were put. But, as Gertrude Stein wrote of the rose, so it may be said, "A rattle is a rattle is a rattle is a rattle."

The passion for noise is easy enough to trace, not only in the average household, but in the world at large. Those that we call uncivilized, the primitive peoples of the world, have always been partial to noise in some form in their dances and ceremonials, peaceful and warlike. Rattles and drums, gongs and clappers, the bull roarer and the war whoop are telling evidence. The whistle, while largely a toy for amusement, came to us from the earliest times, along with the rattle. The squeak toys of the nursery, devised to make sound in a variety of

81

ways, often seem primitive to the ear, even if not in appearance. Yet, when the squeak is gone, they lose their charm.

The jester's bauble with its ribbons and its bells was, for all the world, an idea borrowed from childhood. Somehow, the jesters of Medieval times and those of Shakespeare's day, for all their fun-loving functions, represented to a great degree the light touch of the child in Court affairs. They always evoked their share of laughter, thus enabling many a doughty and gouty noble to exercise his diaphragm, which doctors have long told us was a prime aid to health. And the bauble which they wielded with great dexterity was much like a rattle.

The tambourine has a place too in the list of musical toys, even though it was also used by men and women in various dances in both Europe and Asia. Those wonderful Oriental drums and gongs, with their rich musical tones, likewise remind us of the musical toys of Japan and China. As Mrs. Nevill Jackson stated: "In Japan there is an accompaniment of drum beating at every show, whether it is a peep-show, a marionette performance or the antics of a masked man, or a couple of performing dogs that are being displayed." Sometimes, large drums were set up in the villages, and the youngsters were allowed to beat them to their hearts' content, while an indulgent mother stood by to see that no one was injured.

Speaking of the flute, Mrs. Jackson wrote, "In all countries where bamboo is common, the flute is a favorite among children, for in the ever-useful stems they find a ready hollowed instrument which only needs the holes for the notes and a mouthhole to be made; even the solid end is grown by Nature for the little ones, so that they have but to cut above the cross division and each section makes a perfect flute."

In Japan, on New Year's Day, the boys organize small bands composed of drums, cymbals, and the flute, and go about playing for the amusement of their elders and all who care to listen. This performance is in mimicry of adults who go about as maskers, performing in a similar manner.

"Girl Holding Rattle," c. 1826. Attributed to Erastus Salisbury Field, 1805–1900, Massachusetts.

The Abby Aldrich Rockefeller Folk Art Collection

CHAPTER 12

Toys in the New World

Toys paved the way for friendship in America nearly four hundred years ago. Several elaborately dressed dolls were among the first gifts distributed to the Indians by the English colonists who arrived at Roanoke Island, off the coast of North Carolina, in 1585. An expedition sent by that intrepid adventurer, Sir Walter Raleigh, was led by Sir Richard Grenville for the purpose of claiming some of the New World for England. It had been nearly a hundred years since Columbus' visit, and both Spain and France were already laying their claims to the untamed wilderness. Thomas Hariot, the chronicler of the expedition, recorded, "Wee offered them our wares, as glasses, knives, *babies,* and other trifles, which wee thought they delighted in. Soe they stood still, and percevinge our Good will and courtesie came fawninge uppon us, and bade us welcome."

A gift of toys was bound to make a common bond of friendship, especially a doll, for no other toy says so much by its appearance. When offered as a gift, it conveys a feeling warmer than words, particularly when language is a barrier. What matter the strange and fancy costume — it was a doll! All the Indian tribes of North America were familiar with dolls, and like the early types found elsewhere in the world, they were made of whatever materials could be obtained easily. Wood, leather, and corn husks were typical, and beads, feathers, and homemade trinkets were used to make them colorful and pretty. The corn husk doll is often referred to as having originated with the North American Indians, but it was also a favorite folk toy in various parts of Europe in the fifteenth century and even earlier.

In the time of Queen Elizabeth I, dolls were called Flanders babies, or Bartholomew babies, since many of them were made in Holland and shipped to England, where they were sold at fairs, especially the famous Bartholomew Fair. These "babies" were usually made of wood and, even in the time of Good Queen Bess, had movable arms and legs. Dress was typical of women's costumes of the period, elaborate in its tailoring, complete with ruff and fancy hat, cap or bonnet. A drawing of an Indian squaw and her child, made at the time of the Roanoke Island expedition by John White, shows an Indian squaw carrying a water jug made of a gourd, while her child hugs a smartly dressed Elizabethan doll, which is all the more conspicuous because both mother and child are clad in scanty gar-

84

ments. The attempt to establish an English community failed, but the records and drawings tell us the Indians enjoyed many kinds of sports, including their own kind of ball game.

The children who came to Plymouth and the Puritans who arrived at Salem were not without their favorite dolls and other trinkets of childhood. Despite the hardships endured and the severity of the regulations which were strictly enforced to prevent indolence, some toys were provided, mostly of home-made origin. The daybook of George Corwin of Salem reveals that a farmer came to his shop in 1651 and bought "sugar for the goodwife, and for the children a doll and a bird whistle." The letters and journals of the period were so much concerned with the more pressing needs of life in the wilderness, that it is easy to understand why such items as toys might have escaped mention.

Simple toys and dolls were favorites with the Indian children. Both parents and children used bits of wood and bones to carve toy animals. Nuts, shells, yarn, hollow-stemmed twigs, acorns, gourds, cones from various evergreens, and bits of leather were the beginnings for trinkets of all kinds, whistles, dolls, balls, and other toys. The pits or seeds of fruits, colored black on one side and white on the other, served as dice.

Cat's cradle, that fascinating game played with string or yarn, which has been a favorite of primitive tribes in various parts of the world, was a common leisure-time activity of the women and children of all the Indian tribes. It was familiar also to the English settlers. Many kinds of string figures, in a wide variety of patterns, are possible, once the art has been mastered. When toys were lacking or some new form of amusement was sought, here was a game which two could enjoy to their hearts' content. Scientists have observed this game being played by primitive people all over the world. Many detailed accounts have been written, including a four-hundred-page volume entitled *String Figures,* by Caroline F. Jayne.

Inez and Marshall McClintock, whose *Toys in America* is a treasure house of American toy history, remind us that the American Indians were highly ingenious. "The Pawnees invented a nursery toy similar to the Cradle Gym, which became such a favorite in America in the 1940's. A wooden hoop was fixed to the head of the cradle board, above the Indian baby's head, and from it bright-colored toys were hung, to delight the infant eye and entice the groping hand."

In our preoccupation with the contribution of the English settlers, we often overlook the part played by other racial groups who colonized America in the seventeenth century. Both the Spanish and the French brought their customs and traditions, their toys and their games. In many instances, they probably enjoyed sports and various forms of childish amusement, unhampered by the stern discipline which was part and parcel of the New England way of life.

The Dutch who settled New York had vivid memories of the great fairs in their homeland, where stalls featuring a variety of toys, and particularly Flanders babies, were offered for sale. This was a prosperous period in Holland, and toys were among the many products shipped to England and various parts of the Continent. An old English rhyme of the day tells the story:

> What the children of Holland take pleasure in making,
> The children in England take pleasure in breaking.

85

St. Nicholas, the patron saint of Amsterdam and the beloved hero of children in Holland and other countries, was a benefactor whose annual visit the young folk of New York anticipated with all the fanfare of the Old World. The toy "fairings" which they found in their shoes on December 6 were trinkets they loved. The abundant supply that arrived, each year, on the feast of St. Nicholas at homes in New Amsterdam (as New York was once called) was proof enough that toy land was a wonderful place, presided over by Nicholas himself — a contrast all the more vivid when compared with the complete banishment of Christmas in Puritan New England. The Dutch were fun-loving people, and they introduced many popular games and pastimes to the New World. They had a great zest for bowling, skating, sledding, many kinds of games, golf, and a variety of indoor sports. These included tick-tack, which is similar to backgammon, and trock, a form of croquet played on a table. Many old-folk customs involving hard play were also popular, but not all of these met with the approval of the governor.

The German settlers, who arrived somewhat later to establish themselves in Pennsylvania, brought century-old traditions of toy-making to America. Folk toys which they had known in the fatherland were fashioned with great skill and in infinite variety, for toys were considered important for the pleasure of children throughout the year, as well as at Christmas. The Swedes, the Swiss, the Irish, the Jewish settlers, and other racial groups all brought something of their own as contributions to child life. However, the German craftsmen had an inherited aptitude, and they became outstanding toy makers in Colonial times.

A look at home-made wooden toys typical of those made in the seventeenth century and featured, even today, by the crafters of the Southern Highlands reminds us of the importance of the jackknife. Naturally, few or practically none of the early examples remain, for they were meant to be used, enjoyed, and discarded. Popguns made from twigs of the elderberry bush, whistles from chestnut wood, windmills, water wheels, and various kinds of traps for catching animals were typical of jackknife production. Dolls' furniture from birch bark and wicker cradles and "chaises," or carriages, similar to those used for babies, delighted the girls.

The "play pretties" of the Southern Highlands, which include the mountain areas of Maryland, the Virginias, the Carolinas, Georgia, Kentucky, Tennessee, and Alabama, include a variety of handmade toys whose origin can be traced back several hundred years. They were known by such curious names as the gee haw whimmydiddle. The mechanics of this toy are simple, but why it works as it does has been a puzzler, even to scientists. By rubbing two sticks together, the propeller on the end of one will turn, but its direction can be controlled. Another is the fly killer, made of mountain elder with a piece of split hickory used for a spring. This toy hurls a wooden peg powerfully and accurately for about twenty yards.

The howler, a type of bull roarer, is a gadget that boys, down through the centuries, have found made people "sit up and take notice." Made from a long, narrow piece of thin wood with string or rope attached to one end, it makes a roaring sound when hurled about in the air. This ancient noisemaker is known to both primitive and civilized people around the world. It was used for religious purposes in ancient Greek ceremonies, to round up the cattle at milking time in

86

"A doll's pretty kitchen, stands next on the shelf,
With grate, pans and kettle, and pot;
With dish and tureen, and all crockery-ware,
Knives and forks, and I cannot tell what."

From Wonders of a Toy-shop, *c. 1835*

Europe, as a rain charm in South Africa, and as a noisy symbol in the snake dances of the Indian tribes of Arizona. Other names for this noisemaker are hummer, buzz, bummer or buzzer, swish, thunder-spell, and thunderbolt. Sometimes the bull roarer is notched with tooth-like edges and may have a small hole in the end opposite to the point, where the string is attached.

Another favorite among the southern mountaineers is the flipper dinger, made of river cane, rhododendron stalk, pith from a corn cob, and a piece of wire. Air blown through the horizontal cane forces the light pith ball off its launching pad toward the ring at the end of the twisted wire. A good flipper-dinger operator can catch the pith ball on the wire ring. The resemblance between the rattle trap — another noisemaking toy — and many of similar design which are especially popular at Halloween is easily apparent.

Toy weapons were also fashioned with the jackknife. Clubs, slingshots, air guns, as well as bows and arrows, were the common kinds made. As early as 1645 the Court of Massachusetts ordered that all boys from ten to sixteen should be taught to use the bow and arrow.

The mere mention of a jackknife brings to mind the fact that the term means

a boy's knife. It was the aim of every growing boy to own a knife with a sharp blade of the best steel, for with it he could make all kinds of gadgets, as well as necessary implements for household use. Perhaps not a toy, but it was the implement with which he made many of his own toys and those for younger brothers and sisters. The best ones were Barlow knives, made in England.

There was little, in way of waste material around any farm, that did not produce the makings for toys. Corn cobs, like corn husks, were stuff for a doll and, fastened together, they could be shaped into a fort or a cabin, while the kernels could be used in games. Even the feet of turkeys and chickens held a fascination for children when there was little else to amuse them. Colorful rocks and shells could be had for the collecting. An amusing doll could be made from the wishbone of a turkey or chicken, or, when dried, it served as a bit of amusement to see who could get the larger piece when it was pulled apart.

Dandelions and buttercups, daisies and milkweed, hollyhocks and roses, and many another flower have been transformed into the most fanciful of toys whenever children have been so minded. The flower lore of childhood is a traditional form of play, so old and so deeply entwined in the folklife of many races that origins are not easy to trace. Nor are they important. The joy they provide is brief at best, but this does not concern children.

The blossoms, the fluffy seeds, and the curly stems of the dandelion are the makings of toys galore. The golden blossoms, like those of the buttercup, tell of a child's liking for butter when held under the chin. "What time is it?" or "Does my mother want me?" can always be determined easily by blowing the right way on a head of dandelion fluff. Best of all, the stems make wonderful curls or chains of beads, good enough for any little woodland queen. Another kind of chain, made with daisies, is as old as the hills, and so too is the practice of picking petals off the daisies.

Milkweed pods made tiny cradles and many other fanciful toys, while the silk within them could be used to make the softest pillows imaginable for a doll. Acorns or chestnuts, hollowed out, were transformed into pipes when attached to a hollow stem cut from a nearby shrub. Filled with the dried leaves of sweet fern, there was no need for tobacco to enjoy a smoke.

Toys that packed a wallop as noisemakers included trombones made from the spiny leafstocks of pumpkins and squashes. A whistle that could wake the dead was one made from a willow branch. Blades of broad-leaved grass, placed between the thumbs, needed only the lusty breath of a pair of powerful young lungs to produce the loudest of noises. These and dozens of other toys could be made at the drop of a hat from wayside weeds.

Garden flowers too offered many possibilities, ranging from hollyhock dolls to doll-house toys. Pioneers' children, in nearly every part of the world, have always made the most of whatever was near at hand and easy to obtain in order to fashion toys to their liking.

Skating and sledding in winter, and marbles and jackstones in spring, together with various kinds of ball games, hunting, boating, swimming, and fishing, required little in the way of elaborate toys and provided welcome outlets for youthful energy in Colonial days.

In marked contrast to the messages of good will, expressed in the gift of dolls

88

at Roanoke Island, was the grim evidence which dolls presented at the witch trials of Massachusetts Bay at Salem Village in the 1690's. The former minister, Reverend George Burroughs, was accused of having brought poppets to witch meetings. Two innocent women, Bridget Bishop and Goody Glover, were accused of possessing poppets made of "rags and hog bristles stuffed with goat's hair and other such ingredients." These, according to testimony, were used in various ways to bring harm to others. Such was the part that dolls played in those dark days when dolls were referred to as images, poppets, puppets, and babies, as was commonplace in the seventeenth century.

Among the numerous items listed in "Rates of Imports and Exports," established by the House of Parliament in 1660, were "babies or poppets for children" and "babies' heads of earth." By the end of the century, we read that John Higginson, of Massachusetts, wrote to his brother in England that toys imported in small quantities would sell. In 1699, William Penn came to Pennsylvania and brought a doll to the colonies, along with his furnishings. The traditions associated with this doll have been woven into a story of rare charm by Carolyn Sherwin Bailey in her book, *Toys and Whistles*. Typical of the so-called "Queen Anne" dolls, the costume of this rare treasure bespeaks the fashion of the period. Letitia Penn, as she is referred to, is a cherished heirloom, now owned by a private collector.

CHAPTER 13

Too Much for a Whistle!

By the beginning of the eighteenth century, four generations of Americans had
planted their roots deeply in the soil of the New World. Despite the fact that large
quantities of household goods were imported from England, and settlers from
various parts of Europe were introducing their own goods and customs, many
kinds of local industry were being developed. Yet, the arrival of every returning
ship was awaited with keen excitement by families whose fathers and sons were
aboard. And all the neighbors were curious, too, to learn of the new and strange
cargoes which the vessels carried. It was music to children's ears to read in a
Boston newspaper in 1712 that a privateersman had brought boxes of toys into
Boston Harbor. Every child in the town who could earn a penny or two or had
been given one as a reward for good behaviour would make his way to whatever
shop was offering the new treasures. Thus, the arrival of cargo at every seaport
town in the colonies was bound to produce something new and amusing, particularly if toys were included. Both the captain and the crew, usually, had young
ones awaiting their return, and they seldom disappointed the children.

Curiously enough, Benjamin Franklin was seven years old in 1713. He lived
in Boston, one of fourteen children, and his father was often hard put to it
to support his big family; but somehow Ben, the youngest, managed to get a few
pennies. How the money was spent is told by Franklin. "My friends, on a holiday, filled my pockets with coppers. I went directly to a shop where they sold
toys for children: and, being charmed with the sound of a whistle that I met, by
the way, in the hands of another boy, I voluntarily offered and gave all my money
for one. I then came home and went whistling all over the house, much pleased
with my whistle, but disturbing all the family. My brothers and sisters and
cousins, understanding the bargain I had made, told me I had given four times
as much as it was worth, and laughed at me so much for my folly that I cried
with vexation, and the reflection gave me more chagrin than the whistle gave me
pleasure.

"This, however, was afterwards of use to me, the impression continuing on my
mind; so that often when I was tempted to buy some unnecessary things, I said to
myself, do not give too much for the whistle, and I saved money.

"As I grew up, came into the world, and observed the actions of men, I thought
I met many who gave too much for the whistle."

This bit of reminiscence was written by Franklin on November 10, 1779, and was printed on his own press at Passy, a suburb of Paris. It was part of one of his lighthearted essays, which he referred to as bagatelles. This one was written to his friend Mme Brillon, a beautiful and brilliant figure of the French court, where Mr. Franklin, as "envoy extraordinary and minister plenipotentiary from the United States," had won the hearts of all France by his simple and gracious manner. Franklin's bagatelles were games of delight, literary toys, as it were, written for the pleasure and edification of his friends with a certain lightness of tone. Recently, they were reprinted in *Franklin's Wit and Folly,* by Richard E. Amacher.

Little that was lighthearted in the way of merriment or entertainment was to be found in the early children's books published in Colonial days. Even the crudest of home-made toys or the smallest trinket offered more in the way of amusement. However, as the eighteenth century drew to a close, a change of attitude was apparent in all forms of social life, and the inherited spirit of fun, so characteristic of everyday England prior to Puritan times, began to show itself in many ways. Then, too, the impact of life in other countries was being felt as settlers of various nationalities appeared in larger numbers. The sea captains from coastal towns, who sailed to faraway ports, came back bearing strange tales and equally strange souvenirs to provide new excitement for their families. Yet, all of this activity did not occur within the span of a year or two. The change of attitude was gradual, but it is revealed even in the titles of the children's books. These roving ambassadors were mostly young men in their twenties, and they were eager to learn of the ways and thoughts of other races and nationalities. That many of them were collectors at heart, is evidenced by the rare and unusual items seen in our museums today. Naturally, many of the toys which they brought home were soon broken, but a few remain. Today, even the early children's books are rare collector's items.

In *A Family Well Ordered,* Cotton Mather, the eminent Puritan divine, reminded undutiful children of "the Blackness of darkness forever that was to be their reward." It was not life, but the gloomy shadows of death, that permeated most of the early books for children which, all too often, were concerned with accounts of the passing of "pious and lovely" children. Or, when children quarreled over a rag doll or some other toy, dutiful mothers were likely to quote:

> Birds on their little nests agree;
> And 'tis a shameful sight,
> When children of one family
> Fall out, and chide, and fight.
>
> Let dogs delight to bark and bite,
> For God hath made them so;
> Let bears and lions growl and fight,
> For 'tis their nature to.

However, in marked contrast were these touching lines from Dr. Watts's *Cradle Hymn,* sung as an evening lullaby to comfort babies and small children as they were put to bed:

> Hush, my dear, lie still and slumber,
> Holy angels guard thy bed,
> Heavenly blessings without number
> Gently falling on thy head.

This verse was undoubtedly familiar to every New England child, for it was printed in the *New England Primer,* the most important book in the eighteenth-century nursery. Millions of copies were printed between 1680 and 1830.

Early spelling books and those concerned with good manners, in marked contrast to the chapbooks and ballads sold by peddlers, were either good or bad, depending on the quality of piety, truth, and goodness they imparted. Many chapbooks were illustrated with woodcuts, designed after those published in England at the time. The ABC books, which were developed from the hornbooks, were known in Shakespeare's time as the "absey books," a term which was sometimes used in the early days of the Colonies.

In 1749, an edition of *The New England Primer Further Improved with Various Additions* was published in Boston. It contained such items as the alphabet in several forms, illustrated with woodcuts, the catechism, Dr. Watts's *Cradle Hymn,* verses for little children, hymns, and prayers. Hardly light reading, it contained nothing to suggest amusement or even the mildest kind of pleasure, that was later to be associated with the process of learning. Every school child had to memorize it from cover to cover, or be subject to the master's wrath.

The Children in the Woods, which appeared in 1770, might sound as if it were a charming story. On the contrary, it was a tale of how two children were murdered through the scheming of a wicked uncle. The moral of such evil was duly dramatized in sermon-like fashion. Obviously, the atmosphere of gloom had not yet been lifted. Whistles and tops, cornhusk dolls or a game of cat's cradle, were much more fun than reading books such as this one.

The next year *Tom Thumb's Play-Book* appeared in stationers' shops in Boston. The subtitle indicated that its purpose was to teach children their letters as soon as they could speak, "Being a new and pleasant method to allure little ones in the first principles of learning." Here was a tiny toy book, with pages 3 x 2 inches, referred to by collectors as the snuffbox or waistcoat-pocket size. This was fun! Each page contained rhymes for two letters of the alphabet. At last, stories with true appeal for young readers were made available with the appearance of tales like *Tom Thumb's Folio for Little Giants,* to which was added an abstract of the life of Mr. Thumb. Children could now read about that wonderful character, whom their parents knew as a familiar personality at Bartholomew Fair.

In 1774, an edition of *Robinson Crusoe* appeared in New York. At last, an adventure story for boys, and, of course, girls read it too. After the Revolution, in 1786, Isaiah Thomas, a printer in Worcester, Massachusetts, published *Nurse Truelove's New-Year's Gift: or, the Book of Books for Children, adorned with Cuts.* The title page stated that it was designed for a present to every little boy who would become a great man and ride upon a fine horse; and to every little girl who would become a fine woman and ride in a Governor's gilt coach. Among the stories and rhymes included was "The House that Jack Built."

The very next year, *The History of Little Goody Twoshoes* appeared. It was set forth for the benefit of those

> Who from a State of Rags and Care,
> And having Shoes but half a Pair,
> Their Fortune and their Fame would fix,
> And gallop in their Coach and Six.

It was stated that the original manuscript could be seen in the Vatican at Rome, and that the original cuts were made by Michelangelo. This book, now considered a nursery classic, was reprinted many times and became one of the best-loved children's books of the day. Looking over the titles that appeared in the following years, we find such gems as *A Little Pretty Pocket-Book*. It was "intended for the Instruction and Amusement of Little Master Tommy, and Pretty Miss Polly. With Two Letters from Jack the Giant-killer; as also a Ball and Pincushion; The Use of which will infallibly make Tommy a good Boy, and Polly a good Girl." The long descriptions which were set forth to describe the contents were prepared by the printer, obviously to help sell the book.

Story books for children "embellished with curious cuts" were becoming popular since *The Sugar Plumb: or Sweet Amusement for Leisure Hours* was declared to be of an entertaining and instructing nature, and mention of "leisure" in the title indicates that the "blackness of darkness" had been banished. *Memoirs of a Pegtop* and *Adventures of a Pincushion* were evidence that toys were important enough to be the subject of a child's book.

A Description of the Geographical Clock was a real wonder book. It contained the names and locations of the most remarkable places in the world, and it showed "the time of day or night at all those places 'round the globe," as well as "a copious index." Furthermore, it was intended for the instruction and amusement of youth. It was published in Philadelphia in 1792 for Joseph Scott and sold by Francis Bailey and Peter Stewart. Books like this were even more exciting than toys. Then came *Mother Goose's Melody;* described as *Sonnets for the Cradle.* Each song was illustrated with woodcuts, and Shakespeare's lullabies were included in part two of this ninety-six-page book.

In 1699, John Locke had written *Thoughts on Education,* a provocative book whose influence was to be felt in England and Colonial America for many years. His convictions were diametrically opposed to the stern philosophy of the Puritan tradition, for he believed that harsh discipline and severe punishment were harmful to the formation of young minds, and that learning should be pleasant and enjoyable. While he was by no means an advocate of self-expression, as carried out in some of the progressive schools of the twentieth century, he knew full well the evil influence of too much Calvinism. English children's books of the early eighteenth century were by no means as serious in tone and subject matter as those printed in the Colonies; but it usually took a generation or more after publication before they were reprinted in the New World.

In April 1726, William Price was advertising "children's toys sold at reasonable prices" in the *Boston Gazette,* and a quarter of a century later "London babies, English and Dutch toys, by wholesale and retail." A gold whistle, with bells and coral, was offered at Public Auction in Boston in 1762. Whistles made of gold or silver with a bell and coral attached were never common, and now are choice collector's items. Sometimes, ivory was used instead of coral. These handsomely wrought toys, sold by silversmiths, served as teething rings, but not every child's parents in Colonial times could afford such imported luxuries. Alphabet blocks were known at the time, and as with all the new fashions and trends in England, news of them soon reached the Colonies. They were offered for sale in New York in 1767 — and may have been known here at an even earlier date. "Several compleat tea-table sets of children's cream-colored toys" were offered at the "Three

Sugar-Loaves" in Cornhill, Boston, on November 28, 1771. These references from Boston newspapers are similar to advertisements appearing in New York and Philadelphia papers of the period.

No doubt those itinerant painters known as limners, who went about selling their talents by doing a portrait, a landscape or a still life, were instrumental in

Old New York toy shop.
Courtesy, Museum of the City of New York

attracting children to the art of painting. Colored pencils were offered, along with battledores and shuttlecocks, in 1740. Musical instruments, so popular in Pennsylvania, were to be found in various parts of the Colonies; and for the small children there were whistles, Jew's harps, drums, and flutes, long before the drum and the flute figured so dramatically in the "Spirit of '76," enacted at old Marblehead.

94

The large groups of Hessians who came to our shores at the time of the Revolution, and the English soldiers as well, had some part in providing toys for Colonial children. In diaries and letters of the period, there are enough references to toys to piece together a much more complete picture of this fascinating period. Tin soldiers had been made in Germany for generations when Andreas Hilpert began to produce them in quantities in Nuremberg, in 1760. Because of his skill and efficient method of production, he soon developed an international trade. At first, he made flat figures of molded tin which, when furnished with little stands, could be played with easily. The demand for them in France and England and other countries was great. Curiously enough, during the Revolution, while British troops occupied New York City, the following advertisement appeared in *The Tory Royal Gazette* for December 27, 1777:

TOYS

Christmas Presents for the Young Folks who have
an affection for the Art Military
Consisting of Horse, Foot and Dragoons
Cast in metal, in beautiful uniform.
18 S. a dozen

The price was not cheap by any means, but it was not beyond the means of many of the prosperous families of New York, and these toys were offered at a most opportune time — Christmas, which was a week-long holiday in that cosmopolitan colony. The soldiers were undoubtedly dressed in British uniforms, for Hilpert and his associates had established such a well-organized business that they were making soldiers of many nationalities. Loyalist sympathizers could express their feelings by purchasing these tokens of English power for their children without undue offence, since they were merely toys.

In the days following the Revolution, children in the "New Republic" were playing with toys of all kinds, including "lilliputian dolls," tin drums, Jew's harps, rattles, rocking horses, alphabet blocks, carts, chairs, and other toys. Wigs for dolls were offered for sale in shops, as well as "naked" dolls, for it was the custom for children to make their own dolls' wardrobes. Then, too, dressed dolls were more expensive.

Excavations in remote parts of the world are always surrounded by a certain amount of excitement as to what may be uncovered, but, somehow, when items of more recent date are uncovered in local areas, they often go unnoticed. In 1921, the New York Historical Society reported that the site of a British encampment of Revolutionary times, located near what is now 204th Street and Broadway, had been uncovered, revealing remnants of eighteenth-century toys. Records indicate that some of the British soldiers had brought their wives and children to the Colonies, and the articles found were evidently some of the children's playthings. They included marbles, pieces af school slates, slate pencils, fragments of a porcelain doll, and a toy lamb made of earthenware. Other items found were pewter doll dishes, including plates, platters, a long platter embossed with a little roast pig, a tiny coffee pot, a miniature cup, and a small silver thimble. Toys have a way of traveling, and even though the facts associated with them are not recorded, it is easy enough to trace their origin and thus add another link to the intriguing story of the romance of toys.

CHAPTER 14

Penny Banks

In the days following the Civil War, when tin and iron came into common use for the making of toys, every youngster could follow the development of the rapidly expanding railroad system in miniature, as well as all the latest models of vehicles that were being made in both America and Europe. These metals provided an amazing variety of toys from the cheap tin watches sold in "five-and-ten's" to the most elaborate mechanical figures, such as the dancing darkey, a girl playing a piano, a musical elephant accompanied by a monkey, a fox chasing a duck, and many more. Mechanical banks became all the rage, and so did every imaginable kind of novelty in the world of toys. Since they were being mass produced, prices were moderate. The introduction of electric trains eventually led to the popular fad for miniature railroads to amuse Dad as well as the boys. The story of miniature trains and railroads, *Riding the Tinplate Rails,* has been written in vivid detail by Louis H. Hertz, and the enthusiasm for this hobby has all the overtones of the "tin" soldier mania of an earlier age.

Model automobiles, kiddie cars, bicycles and tricycles, roller skates, and all the rest of the fun on wheels made growing up something of a problem for those who wanted to linger longer in that glorious age from eight to twelve. There was no end to the American toys that were being made, and in such infinite variety. By 1900, there were several hundred toy manufacturers listed in the United States, as well as many other concerns that made toys as well as other products.

What started the wild enthusiasm for penny banks, also referred to as toy or mechanical banks, in the 1870's? Was it a campaign to teach young America to save? Had the staggering costs of the Civil War, so wasteful of human life, energy, and worldly goods, given some New England Yankee manufacturer an idea of using his materials and his labor for a by-product during his dull season? Or did someone suddenly remember the old maxim, "A penny saved is a penny earned"? In 1857, the minting of large copper cent pieces had ceased, and with the introduction of smaller coins to represent the lowest unit of American exchange, tin banks were produced in quantity. These were followed by iron, glass, china, and pottery banks.

In 1870, the J. and E. Stevens Company, manufacturers of hardware, tools, and toys in Cromwell, Connecticut, began to make iron banks with movable parts

96

which handled a penny in a variety of amusing ways and eventually pulled it away from its owner for safekeeping. Three years later, this same company had twenty-one different patterns which ranged in price from $2.50 to $3.00 each. Before the bank-making craze ended, more than two hundred different kinds were made. The simple mechanical contrivances did not possess the refined detail or the expert workmanship of the automatons made in France and Germany at an earlier date, but the automatic action that occurred when a penny was inserted came as a surprise and the question soon arose, "Whose bank is it, mine or Dad's?" Sometimes, buttons from Mother's sewing box were substituted for coins, just to see the bank work. Surely in the desire to demonstrate the newest and latest model, many a penny was inadvertently saved that might otherwise have gone into the coffers of the local candy shop.

Manufacturers' catalogs show us easy-to-identify pictures of these banks made from wood blocks or line cuts, and some from photographs. The treasured relics in museums and private collections are much more real. But until these old-time mechanical toys are seen in action, they have little appeal. Insert a cent or two in the slot and watch what happens. They still have appeal to collectors who seek them out avidly, and some types that are being reproduced now have a ready sale in gift shops and department stores.

In an old issue of *Antiques,* Willard Emerson Keyes wrote nostalgically of the days when penny banks "reposed on the mantel — the carved, white marble mantel of mid-Victorian years — the mantel which never knew the glow of a cheerful blaze upon the hearth beneath. Perhaps it rested on the whatnot in the corner, facing those delirious forms in sable haircloth and tortured black walnut which

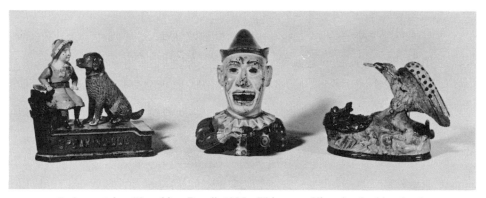

Left to right: "Speaking Dog," 1885. This very Victorian-looking bank probably was an outcome of the talking dog stories. A coin placed on the plate in the girl's hand is deposited in a trap door in the bench. The sitting dog wags its tail and opens its mouth to talk. "Humpty Dumpty Bank." Made in Buffalo, New York, in 1882. The coin is placed in the clown's hand. When the lever on his back is pressed, he raises his hand and the coin slides down his throat. He enjoys the meal and closes his eyes with pleasure. "The Eagle Bank." Made at the Stevens Foundry at Cromwell, Connecticut, in 1883. The coin is placed in the eagle's mouth. The lever under her wing is pressed. She leans forward, flaps her wings, and drops the coin into the slot under her eaglets. They rise up and open their little beaks.

The Rushford Collections

97

Since pottery banks were inexpensive, they were often broken when money was needed. Hence, they are not too common. Maude must have been a very careful girl to have kept it in such good condition. The pottery jug bank is a direct descendant of the earliest type of small-money savers. The Greeks used pottery banks long before the Christian era.

The Rushford Collections

seemed to the eyes of their generation to establish a standard of beauty in household furniture that should endure to be the envy and despair of all posterity to come; but it was there — childhood's penny bank."

Because mechanical banks have a strange fascination for those who collect them, and usually the hobby is pursued avidly by private collectors and savings banks, many of the scarce items have brought exceedingly high prices, ranging from twenty to twelve hundred dollars. This was the price range for banks in the collection of Walter P. Chrysler, which was sold in the 1950's.

Mechanical banks commemorate a number of public figures of the day in such a way that these people will never be forgottten as long as any of the cast-iron banks are preserved. The bank known as "Tammany" is the figure of a little fat man which represents "Boss Tweed" in his palmy days. When a coin is placed in

Wartime banks. America's wars left their imprint on the design of penny banks. The drum-shaped bank is decorated with patriotic emblems of the Civil War, while the tin hat dates from the Mexican border dispute. Ornate tin banks like the Victorian house are seldom found today. They were more expensive than the simpler designs made of tin, and not so many were made. The wooden penny bank was made in England.

The Rushford Collections

his right hand, it drops into his pocket and he nods his head as a thank you. "Teddy and the Bear" represents Theodore Roosevelt, who, while on a hunting expedition in Mississippi, refused to shoot a bear cub. He shoots into the tree trunk and the bear pops out from the top of the stump. This is the essence of the Teddy Bear incident told in Chapter Seventeen. "Uncle Tom" of Harriet Beecher Stowe fame receives the coin on his tongue, while "Uncle Sam" accepts money that is dropped into his carpet bag and, dressed in full regalia, he leans on his umbrella.

"Always Did 'Spise A Mule," also called "The Kicking Mule," portrays a colored man sitting on a bench in front of a mule. As the spring is released, the mule turns completely around, kicking the man over the bench backwards — and

Left to right: "Uncle Sam Bank," patented in 1886. A coin is placed in the outstretched hand and the lever pressed. Uncle Sam then slips the coin into his carpetbag and nods his head as "thank you" while his goatee bobs up and down. "Punch and Judy Bank." With money in the bank, even Punch would have had a better disposition. The coin is placed in Judy's dustpan and the lower lever pressed. Punch does not like this and makes a swing at Judy. She dodges and the coin flys under the curtain and into the back room. "Lion and Monkeys," 1882. The lion has chased two monkeys up a tree trunk. When he attempts to climb up after them, the little monkey jumps onto the back of the larger one (which is missing) and the latter throws a coin into the lion's mouth.

The Rushford Collections

the coin falls into a receptacle under the bench. Other banks feature acrobats, bears, dogs, boys stealing watermelons, buffaloes, a cat chasing a mouse, clowns, elephants, monkeys, owls, and rabbits. "Santa Claus at the Chimney," "Old Woman in Shoe," "Humpty Dumpty," "Punch and Judy," "Help the Blindman," and on and on it goes, to nearly 250 named banks which are illustrated and described in *A Handbook of Old Mechanical Penny Banks,* by John D. Meyer.

CHAPTER 15

Santa Claus Takes Over

Santa Claus is so much a part of early childhood that children usually think of him as an old friend who lives near the North Pole and pays an annual visit to boys and girls everywhere with the aid, of course, of countless helpers, all dressed alike. That he came to America with the Dutch who settled New York in the seventeenth century is known to all who remember Washington Irving. But his story and his heritage are much more ancient. Perhaps it doesn't matter whence he came or how he arrived originally, for he is so dominant and popular a personality in the realm of childhood that only what he brings is remembered. Actually, Santa Claus's popularity in America stems from a poem written in 1822 by a New York clergyman, Dr. Clement C. Moore, for the amusement of his children.

In 1809, Washington Irving had told the story of St. Nicholas in his *Knicker-bocker History,* for the delight of readers in England and America. Some time later, in 1821, a small juvenile was published in New York called *The Children's Friend*. It was a simple book, with eight sparkling color plates and an equal number of verses about "Santeclaus," who was shown riding in a sleigh drawn by a single reindeer. This is believed to be the first mention of Santa's reindeer and sleigh, as we know them today.

Undoubtedly, Dr. Moore had read Irving's book, for it became popular at a time when there were few American writers, and he may have been familiar with *The Children's Friend.* At any rate, he wrote "A Visit from Saint Nicholas," one of the best-loved and most widely quoted poems ever produced in America. Yet, at the time, he thought it of little merit. To a scholar of Hebrew who was working on a dictionary in that language, a man who was also a distinguished Episcopal preacher and the son of the Bishop of New York, it probably seemed like doggerel. It was simply a bit of verse to delight his own children, and the story was based on his own family and their surroundings.

Clement Moore's St. Nicholas was no austere saint, such as was portrayed in the Old World Dutch tradition by Washington Irving. Rather, he was a jolly fat man, typical of the prosperous Dutch burghers who had settled New York nearly two centuries earlier. In fact, this inimitable characterization may well have been inspired by a real person, whose name was Jan Duyckinck. He was the caretaker at the Moore home in New York, and it is claimed that he was "fat, jolly, and bewhiskered" and that he smoked "a stump of a pipe." Dr. Moore's St. Nicholas had eight reindeer, each with a name, to enable him to get around in his wonderful sleigh.

"The Night Before Christmas," as the poem is fondly referred to, would surely have been forgotten or lost, had it not been for Miss Harriet Butler, the daughter of a clergyman from Troy, New York, who was visiting the Moores that Christmas and heard the clergyman read his poem. She got permission to copy it in her album and, the following year, it appeared anonymously in *The Troy Sentinel*, just before Christmas. However, it was not until 1837, when it appeared with a collection of local poetry in book form, that Dr. Moore acknowledged that he was the author. Curiously enough, that same year Robert W. Weir, professor of art at West Point, painted a portrait of Santa Claus, fat and jolly, about to go up a chimney after filling the stockings he found there.

The story of Santa's phenomenal rise to fame in the years that followed and his versatility in meeting the requests of children all over the world have been told in scores of books. However, there is more to the story of this wonderful poem. During the latter years of his life, Dr. Moore lived in a large, rambling farmhouse in Newport, Rhode Island — which is still standing. Each year at Christmas since 1954, James Van Alen, a native of this historic community, has presented a dramatic reading of "A Visit from St. Nicholas," assisted by his wife and four children from the neighborhood. Dressed in costumes of the period, the group assembles in front of the fireplace of the Newport house for the reading of the poem. Then it is re-enacted in the yard, under floodlights, for the pleasure of the neighbors, followed by carol singing. Later, gifts from the sleigh, which arrives on a float, are distributed to a local children's home. Jimmy Van Alen, as he is popularly known, has organized the House of Santa Claus Society, and hopes to be able to raise enough funds to make the Moore house a historic shrine and Christmas Museum. This enthusiastic champion of Dr. Moore believes that no American has provided more joy for young and old. Mr. Van Alen has written a sequel of seventeen couplets to the poem, because, as a child, he thought the poem ended too soon, and he wanted "to make the fun last longer." In an interview with Charles D. Rice, he added, "I used to worry about Father, standing there by the open window as the poem closes. I was afraid he might catch cold, so now I've tucked him safely into bed. I hope Dr. Moore isn't cross at me."

The name "Santa Claus" came from the Dutch *Sinter Klass,* which, in turn, came from *Saint Nicholas,* whose name and fame had been known to every European child for centuries. Nicholas was Bishop of Myra in the fourth century. He was a bringer of gifts on his feast day, December 6, some three weeks before Christmas. His fame spread over Europe in the Middle Ages, and the strange story of his life was told and retold. He became the patron of cities and whole countries, as well as of bakers, merchants, and sailors. Most of all, he was the beloved inspiration of children, for he was their special patron.

Orphaned at an early age, Nicholas decided, when he became a young man, to dedicate his life to God by aiding the poor and unfortunate. Great and numerous were his acts of kindness, always carried out without fanfare or display, and often his identity was not known. His travels took him to the Holy Land and, finally, when his greatness was discovered, he was made Bishop of Myra. In those

101

early days, many Christian leaders were persecuted, and Nicholas was among them; but he survived to return to his bishopric, where he continued his saintly life and his abounding charity. After his death, a great church was built in his memory, and because of his noble deeds, there was widespread devotion to him, and his feast was observed annually.

The story of St. Nicholas has been associated with children for so many centuries that it is no wonder that he became the center of many fabulous stories, and even one in which he conquered the Devil. In the Middle Ages, students of theology used to have favorite amusements during the Christmas season, when one among them was chosen as the "boy bishop." On December 27, the eve of the feast of the "Holy Innocents," the boys gathered in the church, all decked out in ceremonial robes, and conducted a service. After the service, they were free for a day of fun on December 28, which was known as the Feast of Fools. In the thirteenth century, the observance of the bishop's day was moved to December 6, the feast of St. Nicholas, and it became the custom to hold a similar ceremony at his altar in many of the great churches of Europe. As time passed, the procession walked through the streets of the town. In many communities, the boys were given presents, such as cake, cookies, fruit, and honey. Later, gifts of money were presented; and, as might be expected, the school boys made it a practice to go from house to house singing, where they were given gifts of food and money.

It was not long before parents took over the observance, and St. Nicholas was being portrayed as a stern man with a rod, who came to reward the virtuous and punish the "bad" children. In almost every village, one of the fathers would impersonate him in costume and visit each household to quiz the children about their catechism and their Bible history. The story is told that children in northern Germany used to keep track of their good deeds by making notched sticks that served as records of how often they said their prayers. In the Middle Ages, this very real kind of impersonation was dear to the folk, both young and old, and, curiously enough, this custom has not changed greatly with the passing of the centuries. Since the overburdened saint could hardly visit all of them on his feast day, some of his activities were transferred to the evening before.

St. Nicholas used to deposit his gifts in shoes, stockings, and even little dresses which were hung up in anticipation of his visit. In parts of northern and eastern Europe, it was customary for the children to make paper boats to hold their gifts, in memory of those that brought the wheat to Myra when Nicholas was Bishop there. Jeanne Ancelet-Hustache, in a recent biography, *St. Nicholas,* wrote: "In Syria, up till quite recently, the children made boats which they decorated with flowers, ribbons, and mottoes, and which they took to the homes of their godparents and friends; they then went back to collect them the day after the feast, and found them filled with little gifts.

"More recently still, in some areas, shoes and boats have sometimes been replaced, rather prosaically, by plates. These are filled with hay and carrots for St. Nicholas' donkey. Even today, this is remembered in Lorraine."

In parts of Belgium, in the nineteenth century, children drew lots to see who would play the part of St. Nicholas and his two companions. They dressed in costume and went about, singing a verse recounting one of the miracles of their

102

patron. As a reward, they received sugar, eggs, flour, apples, and nuts as gifts, and these were carried home by the boy "Nicholas" to his mother, while his companions brought wood for the fire, so that mother could make cakes.

St. Nicholas had a donkey which he rode on his annual evening visit, and he also acquired a companion in the form of a rough character, a demon he had conquered. The devil, the root of all evil, was very real to the common folk in the Middle Ages, and they never seemed entirely happy until his lurking presence was associated with everything which they loved. Sometimes, this creature appeared in the form of an ugly beast, but to the folk, he was the symbol of evil and darkness, in whatever garb he appeared. He carried a stick in his bags, and other visible evidence of his evil intentions, to remind disobedient children of what they might expect. As time passed, he rode on the donkey and St. Nicholas appeared astride a beautiful white horse. This evil character, the helper, went down the chimney and did all the heavy work in connection with the distribution of gifts.

The arrival of Nicholas and his helper each year became such an exciting event that crowds began to follow him about. Children, in mimicry of the evil one, began to dress in the grotesque costumes of animals with blackened faces. They ran about clanking chains and shaking bits of metal, making all sorts of distracting noises. Such excesses did not long endure. They were outlawed by the civil authorities, and good St. Nicholas and his children's feast were, once again, restored to a more dignified level in European folklore.

Following the Reformation, many religious folk customs were eliminated, especially those associated with the saints, but the great tradition of St. Nicholas could not be forgotten. It was so much a part of the folk life of all classes that at one time, in Switzerland, St. Nicholas' visit was observed secretly under the protection of darkness. All over Europe, efforts were made, during the late sixteenth and seventeenth centuries, to stamp out this custom "in which so much childishness and falsehood are blended." But all the edicts were in vain! The first Dutch colonists brought their beloved St. Nicholas with them to New Amsterdam, as New York City was then called, and established the custom in the New World. At first, they observed his feast on December 6, as they had at home.

With the many changes that occurred at the time of the Reformation, the spirit of St. Nicholas was transferred to the jolly character who was known successively as Father Christmas, the Christmas Man, *Papa Noel* (in France), *Pelznickel* and other titles in Germany, and finally Santa Claus in America. Christmas, instead of December 6, the feast of St. Nicholas, became the time for receiving presents.

New attention was focused on the Christ Child, the giver of all good things spiritual and material, as the source of the earthly bounty that men sought. In many European countries, children were told that it was the Child Jesus who brought their toys and other gifts at Christmas. The beautiful legend, woven around the eve of His birth, stated that a little child came with His angels to trim their trees and place presents under them. In France, it was *le petit Jésus,* in Germany *Christkind* or *Christkindel,* from which the name was eventually changed to Kriss Kringle. Thus, gifts were known as "Christ bundles" and contained all the things that children enjoyed — good things to eat, toys of course, and clothing which they needed. Also, the gifts were given on the basis of good behavior, and as this old custom was continued, under new auspices, the idea of Christmas as a

103

time of reward for good children and punishment for the "bad" remained as a link with the tenets of theology, so dominant in the Middle Ages.

In picture and in story, Santa Claus became the King of Toy Land, and the master craftsman who directed the making of every conceivable kind of toy in all the toy workshops of the world. His portrait was everywhere, and toy sellers and children alike talked a language that challenged only their parents. Santa brought the toys, and the question of who paid for them meant little to the merchants or to the recipients. And, each year, as he filled his enormous pack, this bringer of all good things always had something new and exciting. By 1850, hundreds of toy shops in America had countless numbers and kinds of toys to offer. Most of them came from Germany, but American toy makers were beginning to produce a wide variety of toys, and manufacturers in other lines were producing toys from scrap material.

During the past century, many changes have occurred, and most of the toys sold in America today are manufactured either in the United States or Japan. Other countries furnish specialties, but the output from Germany is much smaller than it was, even prior to World War I.

However, the spirit of St. Nicholas, the wonder worker as they called him, lives on today, not only as the patron of children in every land, regardless of the name he is known by, but also as the symbol of a great tradition. Despite the commercial aspects and overtones that surround the observance of Christmas today, these excesses, colored by a strange kind of exuberance that has manifested itself in the "biggest," the "bestest," and the "mostest," have occurred in other forms in bygone centuries, as the story of St. Nicholas itself attests.

Dickens' beloved toymaker, Caleb Plummer.

CHAPTER **16**

Noah's Ark, the Sunday Toy

Of all the toys of yesteryear, none met with warmer approval from both young folk and parents than the Noah's arks. Charles Dickens wrote about them on many occasions, and no author of his day knew better the deep-seated sentiments of his readers. He retained vivid memories of his childhood, and his own children enjoyed many of the wonderful toys of which he had been deprived. In that beloved story, *The Christmas Tree,* he wrote, "Oh, the wonderful Noah's ark. It was not found seaworthy when put in a washing-tub, and the animals were crammed in at the roof, and needed to have their legs well shaken down before they could be got in, even there — and then, ten to one but they began to tumble out at the door, which was but imperfectly fastened with a wire latch — but what was *that* against it! Consider the noble fly, a size or two smaller than the elephant: the ladybird, the butterfly — all triumphs of art! Consider the goose, whose feet were so small, and whose balance was so indifferent, that he usually tumbled forward, and knocked down all the animal creation. Consider Noah and his family, like idiotic tobacco-stoppers; and how the leopard stuck to warm little fingers; and how the tails of the larger animals used gradually to resolve themselves into frayed bits of string!"

Noah's ark was familiarly known as the "Sunday toy," a curious way, indeed, to speak of any plaything by present-day standards. Yet, in Colonial America and even late into the nineteenth century, the Sabbath was observed with the greatest dignity and austerity, and toys were put away on that day. However, one toy, or rather one collection of toys, which was allowed was Noah's ark. It had the same important family status in England at the time, as Mrs. E. Nevill Jackson, one of the first English toy historians, observed when she wrote in 1908: "To the grim and gloomy doctrine of Calvin, holding all pleasure sinful, we must attribute the extraordinary modern attitude with regard to the relations between toys and religious observances. In the nurseries of the early nineteenth century, all toys were taboo on Sunday: true, as the day specially set apart for praise and worship, our chief care should be to train our little ones in worship and prayer on Sundays; but to tell a child that it is wicked to play on Sunday is a doctrine abhorrent to all thinking minds."

Actually, the most popular toy in all Europe, and America too, inspired by sacred history was the Noah's ark. It was a favorite of boys and girls alike, from earliest infancy. In Germany, it was commonly referred to as "a box toy, since the animals were usually assembled in a wooden box, as were sets of soldiers, farm scenes, toy villages, and other wooden toys."

In *The Cricket on the Hearth,* Dickens gave us more detail on this favorite toy when he referred to the Noah's arks in Caleb Plummer's room. Caleb was a toy maker, and his comments on the demand for this popular toy in the 1840's, together with his feelings that the figures could be improved in scale and detail, are typical of Dickens' timely observations. " 'There's rather a run on Noah's arks at present! I could have wished to improve upon the Family, but I don't see how it's to be done at the price. It would be a satisfaction to one's mind, to make it clearer which was Shems and Hams, and which was Wives. Flies an't on that scale neither, as compared with elephants you know! Ah! well!' "

Under the observant eyes of somewhat over-indulgent parents, children played Bible games with the animals. Arranging them in pairs, they were paraded with Noah and his family in a long procession around the dining-room table or on the parlor floor, if no company was expected. Then before supper, all the animals had to be gathered up and put back in the ark. Those with slender legs sometimes got broken in the shuffle, and an occasional creature's tail was severed or shredded in the somewhat hurried process of putting-away.

Often, the arks were made more like canal boats than the skillfully designed vessel which, in our imagination, we attribute to Noah. As carved in wood, Mr. and Mrs. Noah were usually depicted bent with age, wearing either long, dark robes or the fashion of the period in which they were carved. Their sons, Shem, Ham, and Japheth, were sometimes dressed in animal skins, while their wives were clothed in garments of a much later period, often in vivid color. They were often so similar in appearance that it was difficult to distinguish the three brothers, and many a childish battle ensued over who was who. But it was the animals that held greatest appeal for the children, however crude they were in appearance. Although they were usually painted in bright colors, some interesting examples survive in natural wood finish. The birds, cats, dogs, pigs, goats, sheep, cows, and other familiar animals were easy enough to recognize, but with the strange animals, such was not always the case. Monkeys, lions, camels, and elephants were easy enough to identify and the comment can be left at that, for the young folk who played with them knew them in another way, and that was what mattered. Arks with as many as three and even four hundred figures are still to be found among those made a century or more ago.

When Noah's arks were first made is not easy to determine, but wooden arks and animals can be traced back to Germany in the late sixteenth and seventeenth centuries. The town of Oberammergau, long famous for the production of religious figures carved from wood, is believed to be the birthplace of this toy. John Evelyn, noted English writer, told of seeing a toy shop near the Palace of Justice in Paris in 1642, which displayed a Noah's ark on the signboard hung over the entrance. Of it he wrote, "Here is a shop called Noah's Ark, where are sold all curiosities, natural or artificial, Indian or European, for luxury or use, as cabinets, shells, ivory, porcelain, dried fishes, insects, birds, pictures, and a thousand exotic extravagances."

107

A Yankee craftsman, Harry Trueworthy, retouches an old Noah's Ark.

The story of the Deluge was one of the notably popular subjects offered in the cycles of mystery plays which were presented annually in various important towns, throughout Great Britain and Europe, in the Middle Ages. Noah and his scolding wife brought many a chuckle when they appeared on the stage. This Biblical story was a favorite feature at Bartholomew Fair. Among the popular performances given with puppets in the sixteenth century was "The Old Creation of the World, with the Addition of Noah's Flood." Alice K. Early reminds us, in *English Dolls, Effigies and Puppets,* that "An elaborate staging of 'Noah's Flood' was advertised by a puppet-master called Crawley as presenting 'Noah and his family coming out of the Ark, with all the animals two by two, and all the fowls of the air seen in a prospect sitting upon trees; likewise, over the Ark is the sun rising in a gorgeous manner; moreover, a multitude of angels in a double rank ringing bells.' " An account of a show given in 1703 relates that "while the floods rose, Punch popped his head round the side curtain and hailed the Patriarch with 'Hazy weather, Master Noah!' "

Just as the wood carvers in many German villages used their skill to carve animals during the long winter months, so many a whittler in the Colonies did his bit in making a menagerie of his own concept for the delight of his children. Some of the best-made arks that have survived from the eighteenth and nineteenth centuries can be traced to the Pennsylvania Dutch.

When paper toys became popular advertising novelties in the Gay Nineties, the Willimantic Thread Company of Connecticut offered Noah's arks with a size-

108

able collection of animals. These paper cut-outs were reproduced in bright colors, with easels attached for display. A verse on the back of each animal read:

> Noah launched his ark on the raging main,
> And saved these animals out of the rain,
> We send them, with kindest regards to you,
> And what they say of *Star thread* is true.

Sunday dolls were sometimes permitted, especially in families whose theology was on the liberal side. The "Sunday" doll was a very special person, who appeared once a week and, always dressed in her very best, was carefully put away at the proper time. As the observance of Sunday was gradually expanded to include genteel forms of recreation, tea parties for dolls made it possible for the neighbors' children to bring their dolls to call. But the idea of any rough play was greatly frowned upon, and such gatherings were supervised carefully to maintain an air of proper decorum.

At an early date, Blue Laws were enacted in Connecticut, forbidding its residents to play any instrument of music except the drum, the trumpet, and the Jew's harp. Of the drum and the trumpet, little needs to be said, but the Jew's harp is hardly known today. This amusing toy, long a favorite at various fairs in England and on the Continent, was sold in many of the New England cent shops in Colonial days. It has been suggested that it had an Old Testament flavor, which appealed to the rigorous worthies who founded and governed their colony on Old Testament theology. At any rate, the Jew's harp was acceptable. Its popular name is derived from the fact that it was one of many items sold by Jewish peddlers and one of the few cheap musical instruments, at that. To the Pennsylvania Dutch it was known as *Rumpel*.

Noah's Ark, the nostalgic Sunday toy.
Essex Institute Collection

Margarete Steiff supervised work in her toy factory from a wheelchair.

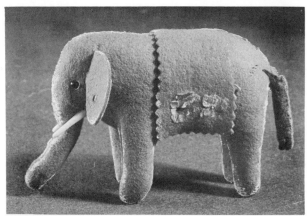

The first toy made by Margarete Steiff.

Street scene in Giengen-an-der-Brenz.

CHAPTER *17*

Teddy and the Bear

More than a half-century ago one of America's most colorful presidents, a nationally known cartoonist, a Brooklyn, New York, toy seller, and a noted German woman, who manufactured toys in a small mountain community, gave the world a new toy that has outstripped all others in popularity. The Teddy bear has probably come closer to being a household idol than any other mass-produced plaything loved by small boys and girls, and parents too. It was not the first popular stuffed toy ever made, but it took first place in the hearts of young and old for several generations, and it lives on as one of the best-loved toys ever made.

When "Teddy" Roosevelt went to Mississippi in November of 1902 to settle a dispute involving boundaries between that state and Louisiana, he was concerned with "drawing the line," as it were, between the two states. The incident has long since been forgotten, but a trifling occurrence, associated with his love of hunting, has made his nickname a byword throughout a great part of the world. Although on official business, he took a little time out to enjoy some sport at bear hunting, but the occasion hardly seemed eventful enough to make much of a story for the retinue of newspapermen who accompanied him. However, the President did set his aim for a bear, which turned out to be a cub, and he refused to shoot the little fellow.

Clifton Berryman, a cartoonist for the Washington *Star,* found the incident appealing enough to make a sketch showing the President's warm humanity. The inimitable "Teddy" was portrayed turning his back on the terrified cub, and the title read, "Drawing the Line in Mississippi." Since the cartoon was reprinted in many papers, the entire nation soon knew about the incident, and like so many of Theodore Roosevelt's activities, it had all the glamour and drama of a very pleasant piece of conversation. At the time, Roosevelt was the youngest man ever to serve as president. His first term in office was as successor to William McKinley, who had been assassinated in September, 1901.

Publication of the cartoon stirred the imagination of a man named Morris Michtom, a Russian immigrant who operated a small toy store in Brooklyn, New York, where he and his wife made stuffed toys to add to their supply of goods. They cut a pattern of a bear out of brown plush, gave it arms and legs that moved, stuffed and sewed it, and used buttons for the eyes. Michtom family tradition has

it that Morris placed the bear in his window with the cartoon, and entitled it "Teddy's Bear." After several of these toys had been sold, the adventurous toy-maker realized the possibilities of his creation, but he was limited in funds. Then too, he needed permission to use the name of the President of the United States on a toy. Permission was soon granted, in a letter from President Roosevelt, who expressed the thought that he did not know how much value his name would have in the stuffed toy business, but that Mr. Michtom was free to use it. Although the Michtoms continued to make and sell their new creations, they were merely operating a small store and could hardly have been considered manufacturers at the time. Then too, the market which they served was limited and far removed from the Fifth Avenue carriage trade. A toy sold in a small shop in Brooklyn at the turn of the century was not likely to create a great stir.

Interestingly enough, the Michtom family enterprise developed into the Ideal Toy Company, one of the nation's leading producers of stuffed toys and dolls today. Because of the exchange of correspondence with President Roosevelt, and a letter from his widow written at the time of Mr. Michtom's death (in which she recalled the request for permission to use the name "Teddy's Bear"), the Ideal Toy Company lays claim to the origin of the Teddy bear. This brown plush bear may not have been the first home-made toy bear that the Michtoms turned out, for the bear had been a dominant symbol in Russian folklore for centuries. It was not new, either, as a subject for toys, since toy bears of various kinds were popular in Europe in Victorian times. But with the appearance of the Teddy bear, something novel in toys was launched that was to have world-wide popularity. English children had always called their toy bears "Bruin," but from the early 1900's the old, familiar name was replaced by "Teddy."

To celebrate its fiftieth anniversary, the Ideal Toy Company brought out a toy model of Smokey the Bear, the firefighting symbol of the National Forest Service. This picturesque figure, known to millions of Americans of all ages through newspapers, movies, and television, has had a very solid influence throughout the nation in pointing up the importance of conserving our vanishing timberlands. And no president of the twentieth century was more concerned with conservation than Theodore Roosevelt.

The Berryman cartoon had obviously left its imprint, for it is claimed that a toy importer took the cartoon to Germany and showed it to Margarete Steiff, a manufacturer of stuffed toys in a small town in Würtemburg, and asked her to make a toy bear for him. Another account relates that the Steiff firm exhibited bears at the Leipzig Fair in 1903. These attracted an American merchant, who imported them and gave them the name "Teddy bears."

Steiff stuffed toys were already famous in the toy markets of Europe and America, and were widely known as playthings of quality. A bear designed by a master craftsman and made of plush mohair, which had the soft texture of the angora goat fur from which it was produced, was bound to attract attention, especially when displayed in fashionable toy shops in New York. The bear made a hit that started a craze, and the credit for it was undoubtedly due to Margarete Steiff, who lived in Giengen-an-der-Brenz in the foothills of the Swabian Mountains in Germany. She was born in 1847 and was crippled by polio at the age of two-and-a-half. Because of her handicap, she became a seamstress, carrying on

112

her work from a wheelchair. In her spare moments she made comical little elephants out of odd bits of colored cloth. She delighted in giving her handiwork to the young children of the neighborhood, and needless to say, every new creation from her deft fingers was greeted with rapturous delight. Soon her quaint animals became the rage in this little Würtemburg town, and even grown-ups sought them for use as pincushions. Margarete's brother suggested that she take some of her elephants to the annual fair in a nearby town, and they were eagerly bought up. Thus, a business was launched in 1880, bearing the name of the thirty-three-year-old invalid.

When she died in 1909, Margarete Steiff bequeathed to her family a flourishing business built on standards of top quality of design and craftsmanship that was widely known in both Europe and America.

The ability to inject personality into a toy and to give it a lifelike quality and an appeal that endures, not for a season or two but for a generation, is a rare talent. Such a toy becomes an inseparable part of childhood, and memories of it are carried through life. Little did she realize the impact of her creation when she fashioned that first bear out of mohair plush — a jolly little creature with movable arms and legs. This little brown bear brought her international fame before she passed away, and kept hundreds of women busy cutting, sewing, and stuffing these cuddly toys.

A visitor to her factory in 1911 wrote: "What had hitherto been a hobby pursued in leisure now became a serious undertaking, and Margarete Steiff showed herself equal to the occasion. Novelty of idea is of course the life and soul of every kind of applied art, but it can only attain significance when, in addition to artistic feeling, the peculiar character and limitations of the raw material employed are borne in mind." Her nephew Richard, trained in the art field, served as designer for the firm, and with his aid she turned out a number of stuffed toys, including a comical monkey, a whimsical kitten, an awkward puppy, a majestic lion, an almost life-size St. Bernard dog, rabbits, pigs, and all sorts of feathered creatures. Each was reproduced with striking accuracy, and the naturalness of these animals, made of soft felt or silky plush, was all the more appealing because of the suppleness of their limbs. They could be made to assume almost any kind of position, and, being unbreakable, they came to be boon companions and playfellows of little folk everywhere. Soon the bears learned to growl and the cats to mew, and if a little pig's ear were pinched it made him squeak. By 1912, nearly two thousand people were engaged in making these famous toys.

Today, Jumbo the Elephant, Slo the Turtle, Snobby the Poodle, Nosy the Rhinoceros, along with dozens of other favorites totaling more than five hundred different kinds of stuffed toys, are shipped around the world from the firm of Margarete Steiff. The rare charm and warm appeal of these handmade animals has resulted in an unusual kind of prestige for the Steiff family, placing their work almost in the realm of collectors' items in the United States and Western Europe. "Cute" is the word that best describes them, and this characterization may be applied to those of miniature form as well as to the life-size gorillas or Teddy bears, dinosaurs and other large-scale toys produced by this renowned firm.

Knopf im Ohr (button in the ear) became the Steiff trademark. From the very beginning, the Steiff toys were recognized for their individuality, and the sense of

113

pride in craftsmanship as expressed in the company's current trade catalog speaks for itself. "Steiff animals look lost and forlorn if placed amidst other toys." Without attempting to discredit any of the claims made as to the origin of the Teddy bear, it can be said that the Steiff bears, which were copied and adapted in various ways, had a tremendous influence on the toy industry as a whole.

Actually, the Teddy bear story has many facets, since toy manufacturers in America, Germany, and England began to produce stuffed bears in enormous quantities in 1905. By the time Teddy Roosevelt left the White House in 1909, production figures were in the millions, and various and sundry claims were made regarding originality and authenticity. As advertisements appeared in newspapers and magazines, the demand grew to the point where the craze was launched with all the fanfare of a three-ring circus. A penny bank called "Teddy and the Bear" was offered for sale in 1906. An advertisement in the May 1906 issue of *Playthings,* one of the leading magazines of the toy industry, read, "THIS IS BRUIN'S DAY — The American line of jointed plush bears is the real thing — Polar Bear, Cinnamon Bear, Grizzly Bear — Baker & Bigler, Sole Manufacturers, 77-9 Bleecker St. corner of Broadway, New York City."

Inez and Marshall McClintock, who have recaptured the spirit and the excitement of the Teddy bear lore in their book *Toys in America,* have painted a colorful picture of the craze which "was beginning to worry a number of people — some of whom were worriers by nature — for one reason or another. The most worried of all was a Michigan priest who denounced the Teddy bear as destroying all instincts of motherhood and leading to race suicide. A Mrs. Harry Hastings of New York answered this by saying, 'Nonsense! I think they're the cutest, dearest, best-behaved little visitors we've ever entertained. I draw the line on their going to church, however.'

"There were other answers. A baby-carriage merchant announced: 'Teddy bears may be a menace to motherhood in Michigan, but we are selling more baby barouches than ever before.' And a woman on Sullivan Street, New York, gathered ten of her fifteen children around her and said, 'Tiddy bears, is it? An' shure, more thin half the kiddies on the block have thim little growlers, an' I don't see any signs av race soorcide in this neighborhood. Oi think that afther wan or two more come along to give me a noice, dacint family to bring up, Oi'll git Dinny to git me a noice, big Teddy to kape in the house.' At least, that is what *Playthings* reported."

A New York manufacturer of dolls' clothes advertised, "Everything for the Teddy Boy and Teddy Girl. There has never been anything like the Bear Craze!" Teddy was displayed in a baseball suit, in a turtle-neck sweater, in overalls and even in Rough Rider uniforms, reminding all of Teddy Roosevelt's swashbuckling activities of the late '90's. Automobiles of the time carried tiny Teddy bears as decorations on the side lamps. Joel Chandler Harris' lovable Uncle Remus bear and bunnies appeared on the scene to keep the "White House" bears company. There were "Electric Bright Eye" Teddies, Self-whistling Teddies, Tumbling Teddies, and every conceivable kind of toy, book or game, ranging from a water pistol to a tea set which carried the famous name. It was a great age in Toyland, and Teddy Bear was King!

In the summer of 1907, Caroline Ticknor of Boston wrote in *The New England*

114

Magazine that the Teddy bear "has come to stay, so perfectly is his grizzly exterior adapted to fitting into the many chubby arms which are extended for him." Within four years of his introduction to the toy world, every child had one. Even then, the Teddy bear was considered "an undying toy personality," for he had proved himself as a make-believe person who could be the best of rough-and-tumble companions. He could be bumped and thumped and tossed about without showing any ill effects. As Miss Ticknor expressed it: "Never before was a playbear so truly and satisfactorily bear-like. There have been woolly bears, and flabby, stuffed-out reproductions, and here and there elaborate fur bears with costly works inside of them . . . But bears like these were never dear, companionable bears. Either they were too fine and too expensive, or they were such as to evoke scornful rejection from the child critic whose education in bear-lore had become tolerably advanced.

"Not so the Teddy bear. He is not only bear-like enough to lift him above juvenile criticism, but he is possessed of those semi-human attributes which fit him eminently for youthful companionship. He is every inch a bear, and yet he certainly embodies exactly the doll qualities which are demanded by the child of to-day. He is well made and set up. His head really turns round, and his legs are nicely adjustable. He has, moreover, that precious gift of true adaptability; he can be made to crawl, climb, stand, or sit, and in each pose he is not only delightfully himself, but he also suggests to the imaginative owner whatever special being his fancy would have 'Teddy' personify."

Despite the popularity of this new toy, not everyone was happy about it. Doll manufacturers feared that the craze would ruin their business. Serious-minded citizens thought it almost an ill omen. Editorials began to appear in some journals, because women carried Teddy bears about with them. In European salons this fad was looked upon as childish, or at least strange, and Americans were looked upon as lacking in maturity. Yet, in Germany the Teddy bear craze created so much business that in 1907 the toymakers of Sonneberg in the Thuringian Mountains were shipping ten thousand Teddy bears to America each week during their busy season — and Sonneberg was only one of the great toymaking towns.

The test of a great toy is one that has what merchants call "play value." Such a toy appeals to the child's imagination, but it must also have in itself some indefinable imaginative quality that attracts a child and holds his interest. That a toy of proven worth must be sturdy and safe to play with is a fact taken for granted, and its eye-appeal is a prime factor, too. The Teddy bear seems to have passed all of these tests, for more than two hundred million of them have brightened the realm of childhood in the past half-century. Usually thought of as a toy for youngsters ranging in age from one to ten, the Teddy bear became a collectors' item with teenagers of both sexes, who lavished as much affection on it as the little tots did.

It is certainly strange that a toy could have such an impact, and become an American legend. Yet, few of the millions who loved their Teddy bears at the turn of the century and in the decades that followed knew much of anything of the history and origin of this lovable bear that has entwined itself in a web of nostalgia and sentiment. Several years ago, a Texas grandmother addressed a letter to Margarete Steiff's American agent, and the firm still cherishes this communication. She wrote: "I have one of the Steiff toy animals, a Teddy bear, which I have had for forty-seven years. . . ." The letter was prompted by the fact that the bear's paws were much the worse for wear, and her pet was somewhat sad-looking. Since she wanted the Teddy restored for her grandchildren, she felt that the company might be able to repair it. "My father bought it for me in 1909. I was then two years old. He also bought me a coat and hat, to match the bear's fur. . . . Through the years, I have loved this bear more than any other toy I ever had — it survived my dolls and all others I played with." Her concluding remarks have a familiar ring, although few have so expressed it. "It may seem odd to make such a request as this, but my bear still means very much to me." She was haunted by

> The battered things that please the heart,
> Though they may vex the eye.

116

CHAPTER *18*

Toys Are Big Business

The manufacture and sale of toys has reached colossal proportions in the United States in the twentieth century. More than fifty million children create an ever-growing demand for playthings, almost from the time of their birth until they reach the teenage class — and even then, there are toys which teenagers crave, although the golden age of pleasure in the realm of toyland is generally considered to be the years from one to ten. For the past several years, the sale of toys in the United States during the Christmas season has reached the staggering amount of more than a billion dollars annually. Interpreted in terms of the individual child, it has been estimated that fond parents and relatives spend an average of twenty-five dollars on each youngster under fifteen years of age.

More than two thousand manufacturers throughout the country produce the bulk of American-made toys. In addition, there are uncounted numbers of craftsmen and small manufacturers who make a variety of products that are not represented in these statistics. Since methods of present-day retail merchandising are highly complex, it is not easy to trace sales in every type of outlet in which toys are sold. However, the Federal Bureau of Census estimates that manufacturers' sales of games and toys in 1960 amounted to $635,322,000.

The sale of toys by itinerant peddlers has long since ceased to be a part of American life, and even those offered at country fairs and carnivals in no way compare with the novelties which were offered for small change to parents and children alike in bygone days. The penny toys of Victorian days have long since disappeared from stores and small shops where they used to be sold. Gone, too, are most of the shops specializing only in playthings. Today toys are sold everywhere, by practically every conceivable kind of retail merchant. Department stores and supermarkets, candy shops, tobacco and drug stores, automobile suppliers, discount houses, stationers, mail order specialists, gift and souvenir shops, and even antique shops are outlets for playthings of one kind or another.

America's oldest toyshop, F. A. O. Schwarz, which also fits the category of the largest and surely the most famous in America, was founded in 1862 and is still owned by the Schwarz family. The founder, who came to America from Westphalia, Germany, built his success on a simple but sound formula. He not only traveled to the great Leipzig Fair each spring to make his selections, but he min-

117

gled with and served both the children and the parents who came to his shop. Thus, he was able to speak the language of children in a way that made his extraordinary selection of toys the most talked-of in America. The story of the business he built is colored with many a warm-hearted tale that has never been set down on paper. The catalogs, folders, handbills and posters which have described the firm's wares during the past century are as intriguing as any picture book of history ever written. Equally appealing are the window displays for which this store has long been renowned.

The fascinating business of selling toys is also a highly complicated operation. More than twelve thousand different kinds of playthings are sold in this great store, and these are supplied from eight hundred different sources. Only about 10 per cent of the toys sold at F. A. O. Schwarz are featured in the company's mail order catalog, which is sent annually to a half-million customers. Each year before Christmas, the sales force is expanded to nearly five times its normal size to meet the needs of shoppers. Recently, an Antique Toy Department was opened, the first of its kind in the country. Most of the collectors' items featured in this new department are arranged in glass cases, suggesting something of a museum atmosphere. Yet, the identifying tag also gives a price for each treasure. The nostalgic tone of the customers' conversations is nothing new to the clerks in this store, but with the introduction of toys of other days, the atmosphere of the Toy Bazaar which first opened at 765 Broadway has been greatly enhanced.

Prior to World War I, three-quarters of all the toys sold at F. A. O. Schwarz were imported from Germany, France, and England. The British Blockade changed the production picture considerably, and to a marked degree indicates the beginning of the marked expansion of the toy industry in America. A solid protective tariff of 70 per cent was established in 1922, which provided further incentive for American manufacturers, and in 1930, tariff regulations were further amplified and defined. The following year, statistics revealed that only 5 per cent of the toys sold in America were imports.

Both the United States and Japan have taken the lead in supplying the demands of the bulging American market. It used to be said that the Japanese could copy anything and do it well, but there is more to present-day Japanese production than the mere talent of imitation. Many distinctive innovations are to be found in the toys produced there. American firms have not limited their factories to the fifty states by any means, and a number of the large toy producers have opened factories in Germany. England is also contributing its share to modern toyland, and so, too, are the Scandinavian countries and other European nations.

Imagination is a prime requisite in toy production today, and in an age when the impact of competition is being projected from many directions, the German skill in craftsmanship is being replaced by what's new and different and very much up-to-the-minute — novelties, as it were. The most outlandish gadget imaginable, presented on television with the right kind of fanfare, sends parents and children alike scurrying to get it. Whether the newest and the latest toys will hold their popularity is not as important as the fact that the demand is present, and it must be met.

The newest and the latest novelty available also seems to be the eternal cry of the buyers who select the mass-produced toys offered in stores throughout the

118

land. Since toys reflect life in miniature and the scientific progress that propels civilization, it is not surprising that Space-Age toys and gadgets are given a big play by merchandisers. However, a rundown of the big favorites among playthings reveals that many of the best-loved and most widely sold continue to have a steady demand and are as staple as a basic grocery list. Yet, nearly half of the toys sold in the past few years show definite influence of the space age. This bit of factual information may seem rather surprising, particularly to adults, who usually prefer to think primarily of toys which they themselves enjoyed. Toy bulldozers, the latest in jet planes, swimming pools, portable listening devices, rocket launchers, and satellites are getting their share of attention these days in a big way.

After several centuries of supremacy in toy production, it is now claimed that "the Germans are sleeping in their fairyland." This nation which gave us the Christmas tree, the best and most distinctive decorations with which to trim it, and the toys to place under it, as well as a major part of the Santa Claus tradition, has long since lost its place in the forefront of toy production.

Scientific experts who project the future of things claim that toddlers fifty years

119

hence will have robots as playmates. It seems strange to contemplate a nursery in which dolls and hobby-horses are to be replaced by toys as extraordinary and precise as the latest and even yet undreamed-of performance of the computing machine. As most of us understand the term, to compute means to calculate, and a machine so named is simply a device to take the drudgery out of mathematics. But, not so with present-day computers, which also include what are commonly referred to as "electronic" animals in the world of science.

The first of these curious beasts was a tortoise, the brain child of Dr. William Grey Walter, which he called *Machina speculatrix*. One of Britain's leading neurophysiologists, Dr. Walter produced this strange creature in the late 40's, and allowed it to roam about his house. Despite its tiny brain, which contained but two cells as compared with the ten thousand million inside a human skull, it revealed strange and complicated patterns of behavior. In describing it in the September, 1958 issue of *Holiday,* Arthur C. Clarke wrote, "It was no mere robot set to perform some definite task, and it was often impossible to deduce, from its actions alone, that *M. speculatrix* was an artificial and not a natural creature. Indeed, it was brighter than many animals, for it could recognize itself in a mirror; and it would bob about in front of the glass until it grew bored and set off again on its endless tour of exploration."

Most of us have forgotten the newspaper accounts of the electronic mouse which mathematician Claude Shannon built at the Bell Telephone Laboratories in 1948. This fabulous creature could find its way out of a maze in the same way that any confused person would try and fail, but the mouse repeated the process with success. It is claimed that Shannon's machine was the first that could *learn by experience,* since it discovered things by making mistakes, but it never made them twice.

The tortoise and the mouse are only the beginning, the experts say, and one has only to watch the latest model of any of the complicated computing machines functioning to realize that the claim is a modest one. Picture an electronic animal with a memory and a vocabulary superior to those of a human being. The idea of a toy machine which can learn and grow like a child, accumulating experience and developing a personality, seems startling. Yet, as Arthur C. Clarke has suggested, "Such a machine may be the central toy in the nursery of the future. It would be a kind of robot companion, matching the intelligence of the growing child, talking to him so that he learned to use and pronounce words correctly, and teaching him the factual knowledge which parents so often fail to provide.

"What would it look like? Certainly not remotely human, for the beauty of the machine seldom mirrors that of the animal world. It might be about the shape and size of a child's pedal car, perhaps with a central turret to carry its various sense organs.

"Balloon tires would give it mobility, but it would probably be unable to negotiate a flight of stairs. It would also be quite hopeless at climbing trees, but what boy ever thought badly of his dog because it shared this deficiency?"

120

Stories About Toys

Stories About Toys

THE MUSIC BOX

One cold December day, a little boy named Carl was hurrying through the noisy city streets on his way to school. Although his coat was thin and threadbare, he was so deep in thought that he hardly noticed the icy wind and the snow which was beginning to fall.

Judging by his face, Carl's thoughts were far from happy ones. This was strange, for he was thinking about Christmas, only two weeks away, and Christmas was usually the very happiest time of the year for Carl.

"But this year," he thought sadly, "everything will be different. There may be no presents, not even a Christmas tree."

Since his parents had died, Carl had lived with his grandparents. Ten months ago they had left their home in Europe and had come to America to live. This was the first Christmas in a new land.

They had been forced to leave their home so hurriedly that there had been no time to pack their belongings. They had landed with only the clothes they wore, and the few things each was able to carry in a bundle. Many things they loved had been left behind. Now, at last, they were safe — but very poor. His grandfather was able to earn a little, while his grandmother cooked and cleaned and mended for them.

They just managed to make ends meet, but there was little or nothing left over and they were only able to give Carl an occasional penny for pocket money. This he had saved. Although he counted it again and again, it was never more than twenty-four cents, and he wanted so badly to buy a present for his grandparents.

He had noticed that as Christmas came nearer they had seemed quiet and sad, although they tried to be cheerful when Carl was by. One night, when they thought he was asleep, he heard them talking in low voices of the happy Christmases they had always had in the old country.

Carl remembered them too — not as many of them, of course. But as he walked along through the snow, he could almost see the gay shops, the flower markets, the toys, and carts laden with fir trees for everyone to buy.

He saw in his mind their own Christmas tree in the living room, trimmed with lovely ornaments and ablaze with lighted candles, with packages wrapped in gay paper, waiting to be opened; and under the tree, the little figures, carved in wood and telling year after year the same lovely Christmas story. His mouth watered as he thought of the good things his grandmother had always made for them to eat.

But Carl's daydream suddenly came to an end. He stumbled, for his shoelace had come untied and he almost fell over it.

He stopped to tie it, and as he straightened himself his eyes lighted on something in the shop window near by — something which belonged to his life before they came to America, just as much as any of the things he had been dreaming about.

He looked harder, to make sure. Yes, there it was — just like the one he had seen hundreds of times in his grandmother's room in Europe but which they had had to leave behind. It was a music box.

Painted blue with golden stars, it had a little Christmas tree on the top and six tiny angels with spotted wings. When you turned the handle the little tree went round and round and the sweetest notes you ever heard played "Silent Night, Holy Night." "Did the box in the window play 'Holy Night' or some other tune," he wondered. Somehow he must find out.

If only he had enough money to buy it for Christmas. His grandparents, he knew, had grieved for the one they had had to leave behind. But the shop was not open yet; besides, he must hurry or he would be late for school. He thought about the music box all morning and at noon hurried back to the shop. Yes — it was still there between the china teapot and the silver candlesticks. Now he must find out two things. Plucking up his courage, he opened the door and went in.

Out of the dimness an old man appeared. He was very tall and thin. He seemed to look down at Carl from a great height, but Carl was relieved to see that he looked kind and gentle. The old man asked what he wanted. Slowly and carefully, because he was speaking in a language new to him, Carl answered.

"How much does your music box cost, please? When you turn the handle, does it play 'Holy Night?' "

"I believe it does," said the old man, "but we will make sure." Stretching out a long thin arm, he took it from the window and gave it to Carl. "Try it," he said. Carl slowly turned the handle.

The little tree began to go round and round and as soon as the first few notes came clear and bell-like, Carl knew it was just like his grandmother's. It played their tune, "Holy Night."

When the last note had died away, Carl asked, "How much does it cost, please?"

"It costs five dollars," said the old man.

"You see, it came all the way from another country."

"I know," said Carl sadly. "Thank you for letting me play it, but I haven't nearly as much money as that." He turned to go.

"Wait a minute," said the old man. "You like my box so much?"

"Yes," said Carl. Then suddenly, he found himself telling the old man about his grandparents and the country where they had all lived. He told him about the music box and the other things they had left behind.

The old man kept silent for a long, long time. Then, at last, he said, "I, too, was a little boy in a foreign country, just like you. I think I know a way for you to get the money. The boy who used to sweep my shop has left me. If you would like to take his place and work here every day after school, I am sure that by Christmas you will have earned enough to buy my music box. How would you like that?" Carl was delighted. It was almost too good to be true. He thanked the old man and went home feeling as though he walked on air.

That afternoon he started work, sweeping and dusting as he had seen his grandmother do. No cobwebs or dust in corners escaped him. In fact, the crowded little shop had never before looked so tidy.

Of course, he could not tell his grandparents why he came home late every day. That would have given away his secret. So they said to each other, "Our Carl is settling down happily here. Now he stays and plays with the others after school."

But Carl was not the only one in the family with a secret. Every evening after supper Grandfather disappeared, and mysterious sounds came from the little unused room at the back of the house. When he came out, he never said what he had been doing and of course, nobody asked any questions.

Then Grandmother, too, had her secret plans. At first she had said sadly to herself: "This year I am afraid there will be no Christmas tree for us: they cost so much. Besides, all the lovely things to trim it with, and the little wooden figures to put under it, were left behind with the music box. It won't seem like Christmas at all." Tears filled her eyes, but she dried them quickly, saying to herself firmly, "It is this Christmas which matters, not those which are past." There must be a tree, even if it is a very small one, she decided.

So, like Carl, she counted the money she had saved — a penny here and a penny there — and the day before Christmas, purse in hand, went out to shop. The trees all seemed to cost a great deal; but at last she saw a little one too tiny for most people. She paid for it eagerly and carried it home in triumph.

When she reached home, Carl was out and Grandfather nowhere to be seen. That was just as she wanted it. She put the tree in the living room and locked the door.

Later, when Carl came in, he, too, was carrying a mysterious parcel and ran up to his room two steps at a time.

That evening, after supper, Grandfather stayed with them. He had a happy and contented look on his face. Each one of the three had a secret which the others must not know 'till tomorrow.

The next morning, Grandmother was busy in the living room behind locked doors. No one was allowed to enter except Grandfather for a few minutes, with something in a box under his arm. Then the door was locked again. In the afternoon, she sent them out for a walk, saying: "Don't come back 'till half past six. We will have our Christmas Eve supper then, as we always do."

At supper time, they assembled in the hall — Grandmother in her best silk, brought over in the bundle; Grandfather, too, was dressed in his best — and Carl was so soaped and scrubbed that his face shone. Grandmother threw open the door of the living room.

Carl rubbed his eyes. He could hardly

believe that it was true, for everything was just as it had always been. Again he rubbed his eyes.

There was the tree trimmed with frosted snow and lighted candles. Under the tree were little carved wooden figures almost like those which they had left behind. So this was Grandfather's secret. How clever he had been!

On another table, spread with a white cloth, were plates of rolls and sausages, spiced cake, and Grandmother's delicious pepper cookies.

All this time Carl had held something behind his back.

It was his turn now. "Please, both close your eyes for a minute," he said. "I have a surprise." They did as he asked. Quickly Carl put the music box on the table and quietly turned the handle. Then it was his grandparents' turn to rub their eyes in amazement, for suddenly into the room came the tune they knew so well. The music box was playing "Holy Night." They looked again and there they saw the little music box which used to stand in Grandmother's room — or at least one so like it that they might have been two peas in a pod.

Carl's secret had been a great success. Two packages which Carl and his grandfather had been too busy to notice were then undone. Still another surprise of Grandmother's! She had knitted them each a pair of mittens of bright warm wool. They were all very happy.

Grandmother's supper was eaten to the very last crumb; nothing was left but the bare plates. Again and again they played the music box. Grandmother found it hard to believe that it was really theirs.

When, at last, they said goodnight, and went up to bed, never had three people spent a happier Christmas Eve.

LITTLE COSETTE

By Victor Hugo

(Adapted by Carolyn Sherwin Bailey)

Montfermiel was a little village in France. There were large houses there, and small houses, and shops, and a little church. It would have been a pleasant place to live, only for one thing: there was no water to be had in Montfermiel — one had to go

a long, long way and fetch it in a bucket from the spring.

In one of the very large houses — so large that peddlers could stop there at night and sleep — lived little Cosette. She was only a tiny little girl, but she had no mother to love her and no one to buy her food and clothes. She took the place of a maid-servant in the house. There were Madame Thernardier and Father Ther-nardier, and their two little girls — Eponine and Azelma — who were happy and gay, but not one of them all was kind to little Cosette.

She was so thin and ragged and un-happy that they called her the Toad. All day long she ran upstairs and downstairs, and washed, and swept, and rubbed, and dusted, and fluttered about, and did all the hard work. It was Cosette's place, also, to go with the heavy bucket to the spring for water, even when it was night; and no one ever said "thank you" to her. Madame Thernardier only scolded her, or struck her for not hurrying faster.

It was one Christmas eve that I am going to tell you about. Father Ther-nardier's large house was full of peddlers stopping for the night, and they sat about the kitchen fire smoking. Little Eponine and Azelma were playing happily with the kitten, but little Cosette was not allowed to play. She sat on the cross-bar of the kitchen table near the chimney corner. She was all in rags and her little bare feet were thrust into wooden shoes. She was knitting wool stockings for Eponine and Azelma. All at once one of the peddlers jumped up. "My horse has had no water," he said.

Little Cosette began knitting faster, but her heart jumped like a big snowflake.

"My horse has not been watered," said the peddler once more.

"Well," said Madame Thernardier, "where is the Toad?"

She looked down and saw little Cosette hiding under the table.

"Are you coming?" shrieked Madame Thernardier.

Cosette crawled out and went for the empty bucket in the chimney corner. The bucket was nearly as large as she.

"See here, Toad, on your way back you will buy a big loaf at the baker's," said Madame Thernardier. "Here is the money. Go along, now."

126

Cosette had a little pocket in her apron and she put the money in it; then she went out, and the door was closed behind her.

Across the road were the shops all gay with the Christmas things. The very last in the row was a toy shop glittering with tinsel and glass and magnificent objects of tin. In the very front of the window stood an immense doll nearly two feet high. She wore a pink silk robe. She had gold wheat ears on her head. She had real hair and enamel eyes. All day she had smiled out upon the little girls, but no mother in all Montfermiel was rich enough to buy her.

Poor little Cosette went across the road and set down her bucket to look at the doll.

"She is a lady," she said softly to her-self. "And the shop is her palace. The small dolls — they are the fairies; and the toy man perhaps is as kind as the Eternal Father."

But she heard Madame Thernardier's voice calling to her: "What are you doing there? Get along, Toad, and fetch the water or I shall be after you."

So Cosette picked up her bucket again and ran as fast as she could until she was no longer able to see the lights from the toy shop and it was quite dark.

The farther she went the darker it grew. There was no one in the streets. At last she came to the open fields, and the darkness seemed full of beasts walk-ing in the grass and spectres moving in the trees. She ran through the woods and came to the spring. But as she leaned over and plunged the bucket down, down, and then drew it up full again, the money for the loaf fell from her pocket and went splashing down into the water below.

Cosette did not hear it. She sat down in the grass too tired to move. Then she re-membered how Madame Thernardier was waiting, and she started for the village again. But, oh! it was cold, the bucket was very heavy, and little Cosette walked like an old woman. The handle froze to her tiny fingers, and the cold water splashed down on her little bare legs. No one but God saw that sad thing — and her mother, perhaps.

Yet, suddenly, the bucket was not quite so heavy, for someone had taken hold of the handle, and a kind, deep voice said:

"My child, what you are carrying is too heavy for you."

"Yes, sir," said little Cosette.

"Give it to me," said the man; "I will carry it for you. Have you far to go?" he went on.

"A long way farther, sir," said little Cosette.

With one hand the man held little Cosette's cold fingers close in his and they went on together. Little Cosette was not in the least afraid, and she told the stranger all about how pretty Eponine and Azelma were, and the hard work, and how she had no mother.

"What do those little girls do?" asked the stranger.

"Oh," said Cosette, "they have beautiful dolls; they play all day long."

"And you?" asked the stranger.

"Sometimes I play," said little Cosette. "I have a little lead sword, and I wrap it in a cloth, and I rock it to sleep when no one sees."

Presently they passed the shops. "Why are they lighted?" asked the stranger.

"It is Christmas eve," said Cosette.

When they reached the house Madame Thernardier was waiting to scold little Cosette for being so long. "Where is the bread?" she cried.

Little Cosette had quite forgotten the bread. She turned her pocket inside out. What had become of the money? Madame Thernardier was about to strike Cosette, but the kind stranger stepped up to her. "Here is money," he said. "When I return I will stay at your house for the night."

Then the man went straight to the street door, opened it, and stepped out. When he opened it again he carried the wonderful toy-shop doll in his arms, with her pink silk robe, the gold wheat ears on her head, the real hair and the enamel eyes!

"Here, this is for you, little one," he said.

Little Cosette crept out from under the table. Her eyes filled with tears, but they shone with joy, too, like the sky at daybreak.

"May I touch it?" she asked, timidly. "Is the Lady mine?"

There were tears in the stranger's eyes, also. "Yes, she is yours," he said again. "To-morrow you shall come with me and be my little girl." And he put the Lady's fingers in little Cosette's tiny hand.

DONKEY JOHN VISITS THE TOYMAKERS

By Margaret Warner Morley

Early one morning Father Hofer got out another sled, for he had left the first one down the mountain, put on his wooden shoes with the long spikes in the heels, wrapped up well and wound the scarf many times around his head and neck. John knew his father was going down to the village and almost fell over with surprise and delight when he asked him if he would like to go too. He was ready in a moment, and they trudged, all three, — for Mother Hofer must see them start, — through the snow to where the gully led down far towards the bottom of the valley.

Father Hofer placed the sled carefully and firmly on the platform of snow at the top. Then he seated himself and John got on behind, his arms around his father's waist and his legs drawn well up out of the way. He had often taken short sled trips with his father down the mountain side near home, but he had never yet gone down the long slide to the village in the valley. He had often come there to see his father start and had held his breath as he saw him flash down and out of sight under the great rock. Then he and his mother would wait patiently for the father to return, for they did not know until he got back whether he had reached the bottom alive. Now they were both going down and the poor mother stood alone with clasped hands and murmured a prayer as she watched them.

John was eleven now and very proud to be allowed to go down into the Toy Valley in the winter time. "Are you quite

ready, my son?" his father asked in a serious voice, and John knew the fatal moment had come. He gripped his father very tight, shut his eyes and bowed his head against his father's back as he felt the sled move; faster and faster it went until John felt as though they had left the earth entirely and were flying through the air. Then came a strange, swaying motion that give him a sudden sick sensation. He felt his father's body sway far out and he, clutching fast, swayed too; then the sled shot ahead again faster than before and John knew the dangerous curve had been passed and that he and his father were flying down the mountain in safety. It is no wonder John almost lost his senses clinging there, for the sled shot down through the icy air with the rapidity of a railway train. In what seemed to John ages, though it was only a few minutes, the speed slackened and, finally, the sled stopped and John raised his head and looked about. They were in the midst of a forest of fir trees whose branches dipped to the ground burdened with snow. The sun was shining brightly, and Father Hofer was looking at John in a kindly manner. "Well done, my son," he said, and John, who was yet so dazed he could hardly stand, smiled broadly.

They dragged the sled after them a little way and then flew down another steep gully, but not so long nor so steep as the first one. Again the sled came to a standstill, but this time only wide, white slopes lay about them.

They were quite below the black fir forest and now they slid easily enough down over the steep open meadows to the very bottom of the valley.

They went at once to the store where Father Hofer left a package of lace to be sent away and sold. There was nobody in the store but the man behind the counter, for in the winter all the people were busy carving and stayed all day long in their own houses. But Father Hofer and the shopkeeper had a long talk, while John looked about the store at the many things it contained, until he discovered a wooden frame filled with carver's tools of many shapes and sizes, and before this he planted himself until his father was ready to go.

John followed through the crooked

street, so narrow now with banks of tumbled snow piled high above his head that he could not walk at his father's side, but had to trot on behind. His father went so fast that he had no time to look at the gay paper toys pinned up in some of the windows, although he knew the children who had put them there. And the broad window sills! — how well they were filled with green moss and bright berries, — though none were prettier than their own at home. Still he would have liked to stop and look at them and at the bright flowers growing in pots in the window where Dono and Peter lived.

But his father went too fast, straight on to the large, wide-roofed, latticed house where the Herders lived. Their window sills, too, were banked with moss and green leaves.

They pushed open the outside door and went into a smoke-stained room like the entrance to their own house. Beyond this was another room, larger than theirs, with a big brick stove in one corner, and here Mr. and Mrs. Herder and three of their children were sitting at a long wooden table at work.

They all got up when John and his father entered. They were glad to see them and had many questions to ask about the health of the family and how the winter was going up on the mountain. Then they sat down and the Herders took up their work again while the visitors looked on and the talk continued. Mr. and Mrs. Herder sat opposite each other, each with a stick of wood clamped to the table in front, against which they held the bit of wood they were cutting, and into which the tool struck when it glanced off. They were carving little wooden horses and doing it very quickly. The oldest boy made the first cuts in the rude block. Father Herder finished hewing out the form and then passed it along to Mother Herder, who, with her small, sharp tools, quickly and neatly separated the hind legs, smoothed and shaped them, cut down the front legs until they were slender and shapely, modelled the ears, the nose, the neck, until the little horse, no larger than your hand, looked quite alive. Then she passed it to Henrico, a boy about Anton's age, who, with a little tool, made some long, fine lines to represent the mane.

John went and stood behind Henrico. He longed to take the little tool and try, but he only said, "It looks easy to do."

"Yes," said Henrico, proudly, "I learned it all this winter. When I first tried, the lines went crosswise and looked not at all like a horse's mane. But, now see," and he moved the tool very quickly, and the shavings rolled out and the mane grew under his skilful touch in quite a wonderful way.

"It looks so easy," said John, at last, "I wish I could try."

"No, no," said Mother Herder, anxiously, "you would spoil the wood and maybe break the tool. It takes practice."

"John wants to carve," said Father Hofer, "but I tell him it is folly, for none of our family has ever carved."

He said this a little sadly, for it was a great honor in the Toy Valley to be able to carve.

"I am going to carve," came a piping voice, apparently from the roof. John looked around and saw little Hans peeping down at him from the bed made on the platform above the stove. He had gone up there to take a nap because it was so warm. All the children laughed, for little Hans was a great pet.

John looked enviously at the young Herders who sat busy at the table with their parents. They were all doing some part of the work on the horses and the youngest of them was no older than John himself. When he got tired of watching the busy fingers perform the work that looked so easy, his eyes wandered about until, through an open door which led into another room, he saw piles and piles of horses apparently all finished. Finally, he went and stood in the doorway and looked at them.

In a few minutes his father got up, said good-bye to the family, and again went out into the sparkling, white world, along a lane that led them out of the village, down across a bridge over a little stream that made a loud and pleasant sound as it rushed along between its ice-bound banks.

They followed a path across some meadows, quite across the valley to a little stone house under the shadow of the opposite mountain. Here a thread of water had been led close to the house wall; but the shining thing rushed as swiftly as the larger stream, for it, too, came down from the high glaciers, and was in a hurry to join the other and rush with it down the valley and through the long and narrow gorge that shut up the valley from the outer world, and into the great river that hurried, ever hurried, down out of the mountains and across the plains to lose itself in the waters of the blue Adriatic.

In this house lived Father Hofer's old friend Ampezzang. Again they went through a dark, smoke-stained room into a little one beyond where stood the big brick stove. There was never any smoke stain in this inner room because there was not even a stove pipe in it, for you must know that the stove opened into the outer hallway where the fire was made, the fuel put in, and the big brick vault thoroughly heated.

Ampezzang and his wife and son were at work in the inner room. Herr Ampezzang sat alone at a little table on which was a lathe turned swiftly by the rushing brook outside, and by means of which Herr Ampezzang was cutting out toy wagon wheels at a great rate.

The wife and son were fitting little spokes into the wheels, a task that looked very easy, indeed. But when Frau Ampezzang put a wheel rim and some spokes into John's hand and told him to try it, he could not do it at all. First, the rim flew across the room, then he broke the spoke he was trying to force into place. Young Ampezzang laughed, but Frau Ampezzang, seeing how red John's face became, looked kindly at him and said it didn't matter, they had plenty of the little spokes and some of them were often broken.

"He has a notion that he wants to carve," said Father Hofer, shaking his head, "but I know he never could learn."

"Bless the child!" cried Frau Ampezzang. "Of course he could learn. It is just wanting to hard enough and keeping at it long enough," and she smiled so kindly that John had a sudden warm feeling at his heart and his blue eyes shone with pleasure.

When they were leaving Frau Ampezzang looked at John and said again, very slowly and in a tone he never forgot, "It is just wanting to hard enough and keeping at it long enough."

129

John would have liked to stay there close to kind Frau Ampezzang all day, but his father soon took leave and they went next to see the Wolferlos, who lived at the foot of the steep bluff on top of which stood a tiny, close village and a church with a tall spire.

Here the whole family were painting wooden horses. Two lads painted them white and set them aside to dry. The others took the white horses that had already dried and painted black spots on them and a black stripe down their backs: though, why they did this I cannot tell you and I doubt if they could have told themselves. Certainly no living white horse ever had such spots on it or such a line down its spine. But horses were scarce in the Toy Valley and probably no one in it had ever seen a white horse, and so they had to do the best they could, and once, away back, no doubt some carver with a bright imagination had so painted his horses and ever after all his descendants, who knew no more about white horses than he did, had painted them that way too. Anyhow, there they were and they remind me of an elephant I once saw in Spain. Not a live elephant, of course, for live elephants are not common in Spain. In fact, they are about as uncommon as white horses were in those days in the Toy Valley. They have come in since, — white horses, I mean, — for a road has been built up the eight-mile ravine that connects the Toy Valley with the rest of the world, and now you can ride in there on a stage coach, if you like, with any number of white horses. But the people still paint the toy horses the way they used to!

But about that elephant — let me see! Oh, yes! It was in Spain and it was made of china. It was quite an elephant, all but one thing. Whoever made it was not as familiar with elephants as you are who can go to the zoological garden any time you like, and no doubt have ridden on one.

Well, when the Man Who Was Not Familiar With Elephants was ready to put in the nose he didn't know where it went. Of course *you* know that the elephant's nose is its trunk. It *is* long, but it is a nose all the same. And that he can pick up peanuts with it I am well aware. Still, it

130

is a nose and it opens as anybody's nose does, at the end in two round holes. And that is all the opening it has. The elephant has to breathe the air up through the whole length of that trunk through those nostrils at the end. Now, the man in Spain not knowing much about the elephant's trunk and probably thinking it a sort of misplaced tail, set the nostrils in the front of the trunk, a little below the eyes. That is, he painted them there where nostrils belong, — in every four-legged animal but an elephant. You didn't notice it at first, but after you had once seen them, it seemed as if you couldn't see anything else and the more you looked at them the funnier they got. A friend of mine has that elephant now and any one may see it that wants to.

This reminds me of another elephant story I would like to tell you if you don't mind. Once at the London Zoological Gardens the elephants were carrying loads of children on their backs from one place to another. The children who were walking on the ground would feed the elephants as they passed. The elephants did not have to stop, they just stuck out their trunks and took the cakes and peanuts as they were walking along. Now, one big elephant snatched a bag of cakes out of a child's hand, which was not polite even in an elephant. But he was paid for it, as you will see, for he took hold of the bottom of the bag and as he chewed, no doubt wondering why he could not taste the cakes he knew were inside, the cakes tumbled out at the other end and fell on the ground. Another elephant passing at the moment and taking in the situation, wheeled about, and in spite of his keeper and the children on his back, coolly picked up the cakes and ate them, while Elephant Number One was hopefully chewing on the empty bag.

Now let me see, where were we? Oh, yes, — at the Wolferlos'. The whole family were painting their wooden horses white with black markings, only the youngest child, a little girl younger than John, had some bright red paint and a little brush with which she carefully put a spot in each nostril and also on the inside of the half-open mouths. She was a pretty little thing with her long flaxen braids wound about her head, and she puckered up her mouth in a comical way whenever she put on a red spot, and this pleased John so much that he sat and watched her instead of the others.

They did not stay here long, but visited at another stone house with very deep overhanging porches and broad lattices. The upper part of this building was bulging with hay. The family lived on the floor below, and under them on the ground floor were kept the horse, the cow, and the goats — all very convenient in cold weather.

This family was also at work, even to the old grandfather, making wooden dolls. Not by any means those sticks of wood with a doll's head on top that the babies of the Toy Valley love to hug, — somebody else made *them,* — but real dolls with jointed legs and arms.

"See," said the grandfather, holding out a handful of dolls no more than an inch long, "these are the smallest jointed dolls in the world," — and sure enough, those mites were jointed and could bend their knees and elbows and sit down.

"It takes skill," he cried chuckling, "and the mother does it all. Hers are the only fingers fine enough for such work as that," and he looked with pride at the tiny things lying in the palm of his great hand.

Dolls were everywhere in this room, hanging and standing about that the paint on them might dry, and John came near sitting down in a basketful of dolls' arms, while another one full of leg joints stood ready on the table.

The children were all busy fitting the joints together and fastening them with little wooden pegs, while the father, who had a jolly red face, was boring holes for the pegs to go into.

They were a merry set, these doll-makers, and the children had round faces and round eyes and little pug noses and bright red cheeks and looked very much like their own dolls come to life — and grown bigger, of course. Only they were not a bit wooden, but laughed and chattered and showed John everything they had.

He had seen all this toy-making many times before, but to-day it was different; it seemed some way as though he were looking at it for the first time. The desire

to become a carver had come to him the summer before and now everything connected with it had a new meaning.

They did not stay long with the doll-makers, but went next to his father's relative, he whom they called Uncle Francesco. He had been a hunter in his young days; but now that he was old he stayed at home and worked the piece of land he owned on the slope above the village.

They had dinner here, and as soon as it was over John was sent to the store to get the sled his father had left there and which he meant to leave in Uncle Francesco's shed until summer time, when he would bring Franz down and let him carry it home on his back. He had three or four of these sleds which he used for sliding down to the Toy Valley in the winter time.

When John got back with the sled, his father and Uncle Francesco were talking very earnestly about something, but stopped as soon as he entered the room.

"Now we must be starting up the mountain," said Father Hofer, getting up and beginning to wind his scarf about his neck. It was early yet, but it would take a long time to climb up through the snow and the days were short.

They had no trouble going up the open slopes, for there were paths everywhere made by the people to go from farm to farm, and from their houses down to the village. But when they had climbed above the open slopes into the woods there was no path; only Father Hofer knew the way very well and how to find the least snowy trails under the cliffs, and the long spikes in their shoes kept them from slipping.

It was very cold and very still in the woods, and every little while they heard a loud report which Father Hofer said was the cold splitting the trees. John's breath froze in a thick fringe on the scarf wound about his neck and ears, but inside his warm wrappings his blood tingled and he did not feel the cold at all.

If you had been there you would have thought you were climbing up through a forest of Christmas trees, for each evergreen was hung with snow wreaths and glittering ice jewels.

It was very beautiful, and yet it was a long, hard climb for John, and as night

131

came early they had to hurry. When finally they reached the top and Mother Hofer opened the door and let out a flood of warmth and the fragrant odor of the cooking supper, John rushed in never so glad in all his life before to be at home.

He was almost too tired to eat, but he felt very proud to think he had really been down to the valley in the winter time. He felt as though he were quite grown up and not at all the little boy who that morning had hugged his father so closely. "Soon I shall be able to slide down by myself," he thought sleepily as he climbed to his warm bed above the great stove, and all night long he seemed to be speeding through the air after wonderful toy horses that galloped swiftly ahead of him.

THE WEDDING PROCESSION OF THE RAG DOLL AND THE BROOM HANDLE AND WHO WAS IN IT

By Carl Sandburg

The Rag Doll had many friends. The Whisk Broom, the Furnace Shovel, the Coffee Pot, they all liked the Rag Doll very much.

But when the Rag Doll married, it was the Broom Handle she picked because the Broom Handle fixed her eyes.

A proud child, proud but careless, banged the head of the Rag Doll against a door one day and knocked off both the glass eyes sewed on long ago. It was then the Broom Handle found two black California prunes, and fastened the two California prunes just where the eyes belonged. So then the Rag Doll had two fine black eyes brand new. She was even nicknamed Black Eyes by some people.

There was a wedding when the Rag Doll married the Broom Handle. It was a grand wedding with one of the grandest processions ever seen at a rag doll wedding. And we are sure no broom handle ever had a grander wedding procession when he got married.

Who marched in the procession? Well, first came the Spoon Lickers. Every one of them had a tea spoon, or a soup spoon, though most of them had a big table spoon. On the spoons, what did they have? Oh, some had butter scotch, some had gravy, some had marshmallow fudge. Every one had something slickery sweet or fat to eat on the spoon. And as they marched in the wedding procession of the Rag Doll and the Broom Handle, they licked their spoons and looked around and licked their spoons again.

Next came the Tin Pan Bangers. Some had dishpans, some had frying pans, some had potato peeling pans. All the pans were tin with tight tin bottoms. And the Tin Pan Bangers banged with knives and forks and iron and wooden bangers on the bottoms of the tin pans. And as they marched in the wedding procession of the Rag Doll and the Broom Handle they banged their pans and looked around and banged again.

Then came the Chocolate Chins. They were all eating chocolates. And the chocolate was slippery and slickered all over their chins. Some of them spattered the ends of their noses with black chocolate. Some of them spread the brown chocolate nearly up to their ears. And then as they marched in the wedding procession of the Rag Doll and the Broom Handle they stuck their chins in the air and looked around and stuck their chins in the air again.

Then came the Dirty Bibs. They wore plain white bibs, checker bibs, stripe bibs, blue bibs and bibs with butterflies. But all the bibs were dirty. The plain white bibs were dirty, the checker bibs were dirty, the stripe bibs, the blue bibs and the bibs with butterflies on them, they were all dirty. And so in the wedding procession of the Rag Doll and the Broom Handle, the Dirty Bibs marched with their dirty fingers on the bibs and they looked around and laughed and looked around and laughed again.

Next came the Clean Ears. They were

132

proud. How they got into the procession nobody knows. Their ears were all clean. They were clean not only on the outside but they were clean on the inside. There was not a speck of dirt or dust or muss or mess on the inside nor the outside of their ears. And so in the wedding procession of the Rag Doll and the Broom Handle, they wiggled their ears and looked around and wiggled their ears again.

The Easy Ticklers were next in the procession. Their faces were shining. Their cheeks were like bars of new soap. Their ribs were strong and the meat and the fat was thick on their ribs. It was plain to see they were saying, "Don't tickle me because I tickle so easy." And as they marched in the wedding procession of the Rag Doll and the Broom Handle, they tickled themselves and laughed and looked around and tickled themselves again.

The music was furnished mostly by the Musical Soup Eaters. They marched with big bowls of soup in front of them and big spoons for eating the soup. They whistled and chuzzled and snozzled the soup and the noise they made could be

heard far up at the head of the procession where the Spoon Lickers were marching. So they dipped their soup and looked around and dipped their soup again.

The Chubby Chubs were next. They were roly poly, round faced smackers and snoozers. They were not fat babies — oh no, oh no — not fat but just chubby and easy to squeeze. They marched on their chubby legs and chubby feet and chubbed their chubs and looked around and chubbed their chubs again.

The last of all in the wedding procession of the Rag Doll and the Broom Handle were the Sleepyheads. They were smiling and glad to be marching but their heads were slimpsing down and their smiles were half fading away and their eyes were half shut or a little more than half shut. They staggered just a little as though their feet were not sure where they were going. They were the Sleepyheads, the last of all, in the wedding procession of the Rag Doll and the Broom Handle and the Sleepyheads they never looked around at all.

It *was* a grand procession, don't you think so?

THE GINGERBREAD BOY

(Adapted by Carolyn S. Bailey)

There were once a little old woman and a little old man, who lived in a little old house in the woods. They had a cookstove, with a little black kettle always singing away on it. They should have been a happy old couple but for one thing — they wanted a little child of their own, and they had none.

One morning when the little old woman was making gingerbread, she cut a cake in the shape of a little boy; she dropped it into the pan, and put the pan in the oven. Presently she opened the oven door to see if he were baked, but out jumped the gingerbread boy, and away he ran as fast as his legs could carry him.

The little old woman called her husband, and they both ran after him, but they could not catch him. And the gingerbread boy ran on until he came to a barn full of threshers. As he went by the door, he called to them:

"I've run away from a little old woman,
  A little old man,
  A little old kettle,
  A little old pan,
  And I can run away from you, I can."

Then the barnful of threshers set out to run after him. Though they ran very fast, they could not catch him. And he hurried on until he came to a field full of mowers. He called out to them:

"I've run away from a little old woman,
  A little old man,
  A little old kettle,
  A little old pan,
  A barn full of threshers,
  And I can run away from you, I can."

133

Then the fieldful of mowers set out to run after him, but they could not catch him. And the gingerbread boy ran on and on, until he came to a cow. He called out to the cow:

"I've run away from a little old woman,
A little old man,
A little old kettle,
A little old pan,
A barn full of threshers,
A field full of mowers,
And I can run away from you, I can."

So the cow ran, but she couldn't catch the gingerbread boy who ran on and on, until he met a fox; and to the fox he called out:

"I've run away from a little old woman,
A little old man,
A little old kettle,
A little old pan,
A barn full of threshers,
A field full of mowers,
A cow,
And I can run away from you, I can."

Now, a fox can run very fast. On and on ran the fox after the gingerbread boy until they came to a river.

"Should you like to go across?" asked the sly old fox. "Jump on my tail."

So the gingerbread boy jumped up on the fox's tail, and the fox began swimming across the river. But he had gone only a few strokes when he called back to the gingerbread boy, "The water is deep, and we may drown! Jump on my back!"

So the gingerbread boy jumped up on the fox's back. Then the fox swam a few more strokes and he called out, "The water grows deeper and deeper. Jump upon my nose!"

So the gingerbread boy jumped upon the fox's nose. Just then they reached the other bank. The sly old fox opened his mouth wide and in went the gingerbread boy!

"Dear me!" he said after a minute. "Here I am a quarter gone."

And then he said, "Now I am half gone."

And then, "I am three-quarters gone."

But at last he said, "Well, here I am about to be all gone!"

And he never spoke again.

THE STEADFAST TIN SOLDIER

By Hans Christian Andersen

There were once five-and-twenty tin soldiers. They were all brothers, born of the same old tin spoon. They shouldered their muskets and looked straight ahead of them, splendid in their uniforms, all red and blue.

The very first thing in the world that they heard was, "Tin soldiers!" A small boy shouted it and clapped his hands as the lid was lifted off their box on his birthday. He immediately set them up on the table.

All the soldiers looked exactly alike except one. He looked a little different as he had been cast last of all. The tin was short, so he had only one leg. But there he stood, as steady on one leg as any of the other soldiers on their two. But just you see, he'll be the remarkable one.

On the table with the soldiers were many other playthings, and one that no eye could miss was a marvelous castle of cardboard. It had little windows through which you could look right inside it. And in front of the castle were miniature trees around a little mirror supposed to represent a lake. The wax swans that swam on its surface were reflected in the mirror. All this was very pretty but the prettiest of all was the little lady who stood in the open doorway of the castle. Though she was a paper doll, she wore a dress of the fluffiest gauze. A tiny blue ribbon went over her shoulder for a scarf, and in the middle of it shone a spangle that was as big as her face. The little lady held out both her arms, as a ballet dancer does, and one leg was lifted so high behind her that the tin soldier couldn't see it at all, and he supposed she must have only one leg, as he did.

"That would be a wife for me," he thought. "But maybe she's too grand. She lives in a castle. I have only a box,

134

with four-and-twenty roommates to share it. That's no place for her. But I must try to make her acquaintance." Still as stiff as when he stood at attention, he lay down on the table behind a snuffbox, where he could admire the dainty little dancer who kept standing on one leg without ever losing her balance.

When the evening came the other tin soldiers were put away in their box, and the people of the house went to bed. Now the toys began to play among themselves at visits, and battles, and at giving balls. The tin soldiers rattled about in their box, for they wanted to play too, but they could not get the lid open. The nutcracker turned somersaults, and the slate pencil squeaked out jokes on the slate. The toys made such a noise that they woke up the canary bird, who made them a speech, all in verse. The only two who stayed still were the tin soldier and the little dancer. Without ever swerving from the tip of one toe, she held out her arms to him, and the tin soldier was just as steadfast on his one leg. Not once did he take his eyes off her.

Then the clock struck twelve and — *clack!* — up popped the lid of the snuffbox. But there was no snuff in it, no — out bounced a little black bogey, a jack-in-the-box.

"Tin soldier," he said. "Will you please keep your eyes to yourself?"

The tin soldier pretended not to hear.

The bogey said, "Just you wait till tomorrow."

But when morning came, and the children got up, the soldier was set on the window ledge. And whether the bogey did it, or there was a gust of wind, all of a sudden the window flew open and the soldier pitched out headlong from the third floor. He fell at breathtaking speed and landed cap first, with his bayonet buried between the paving stones and his one leg stuck straight in the air. The housemaid and the little boy ran down to look for him and, though they nearly stepped on the tin soldier, they walked right past without seeing him. If the soldier had called, "Here I am!" they would surely have found him, but he thought it contemptible to raise an uproar while he was wearing his uniform.

Soon it began to rain. The drops fell faster and faster, until they came down by the bucketful. As soon as the rain let up, along came two young rapscallions.

"Hi, look!" one of them said, "there's a tin soldier. Let's send him sailing."

They made a boat out of newspaper, put the tin soldier in the middle of it, and away he went down the gutter with the two young rapscallions running beside him and clapping their hands. High heavens! How the waves splashed, and how fast the water ran down the gutter. Don't forget that it had just been raining by the bucketful. The paper boat pitched, and tossed, and sometimes it whirled about so rapidly that it made the soldier's head spin. But he stood as steady as ever. Never once flinching, he kept his eyes front, and carried his gun shoulder-high. Suddenly the boat rushed under a long plank where the gutter was boarded over. It was as dark as the soldier's own box.

"Where can I be going?" the soldier wondered. "This must be that black bogey's revenge. Ah! if only I had the little lady with me, it could be twice as dark here for all that I would care."

Out popped a great water rat who lived under the gutter plank.

"Have you a passport?" said the rat. "Hand it over."

The soldier kept quiet and held his musket tighter. On rushed the boat, and the rat came right after it, gnashing his teeth as he called to the sticks and straws:

"Halt him! Stop him! He didn't pay his toll. He hasn't shown his passport."

But the current ran stronger and stronger. The soldier could see daylight ahead where the board ended, but he also heard a roar that would frighten the bravest of us. Hold on! Right at the end of that gutter plank the water poured into the great canal. It was as dangerous to him as a waterfall would be to us.

He was so near it he could not possibly stop. The boat plunged into the whirlpool. The poor tin soldier stood as staunch as he could, and no one can say that he so much as blinked an eye. Thrice and again the boat spun around. It filled to the top and was bound to sink. The water was up to his neck and still the boat went down, deeper, deeper, deeper, and the paper got soft and limp. Then the water rushed over his head. He thought of the

pretty little dancer whom he'd never see again, and in his ears rang an old, old song:

Farewell, farewell, O warrior brave,
Nobody can from Death thee save.

And now the paper boat broke beneath him, and the soldier sank right through. And just at that moment he was swallowed by a most enormous fish.

My! How dark it was inside that fish. It was darker than under the gutter-plank and it was so cramped, but the tin soldier still was staunch. He lay there full length, soldier fashion, with musket to shoulder.

Then the fish flopped and floundered in a most unaccountable way. Finally it was perfectly still, and after a while something struck through him like a flash of lightning. The tin soldier saw daylight again, and he heard a voice say, "The Tin Soldier!" The fish had been caught, carried to market, bought, and brought to a kitchen where the cook cut him open with her big knife.

She picked the soldier up bodily between her two fingers, and carried him off upstairs. Everyone wanted to see this remarkable traveler who had traveled about in a fish's stomach, but the tin soldier took no pride in it. They put him on the table and — lo and behold, what curious things can happen in this world — there he was, back in the same room as before. He saw the same children, the same toys were on the table, and there was the same fine castle with the pretty little dancer. She still balanced on one leg, with the other raised high. She too was steadfast. That touched the soldier so deeply that he would have cried tin tears, only soldiers never cry. He looked at her, and she looked at him, and never a word was said. Just as things were going so nicely for them, one of the little boys snatched up the tin soldier and threw him into the stove. He did it for no reason at all. That black bogey in the snuffbox must have put him up to it.

The tin soldier stood there dressed in flames. He felt a terrible heat, but whether it came from the flames or from his love he didn't know. He'd lost his splendid colors, maybe from his hard journey, maybe from grief, nobody can say.

He looked at the little lady, and she looked at him, and he felt himself melting. But still he stood steadfast, with his musket held trim on his shoulder.

Then the door blew open. A puff of wind struck the dancer. She flew like a sylph, straight into the fire with the soldier, blazed up in a flash, and was gone. The tin soldier melted, all in a lump. The next day, when a servant took up the ashes she found him in the shape of a little tin heart. But of the pretty dancer nothing was left except her spangle, and that was burned as black as a coal.

Bibliography

ACKLEY, EDITH FLACK. *A Doll Shop of Your Own.* New York: Stokes, 1941.

D'ALLEMAGNE, HENRI RENÉ. *Histoire des Jouets.* Paris: 1903.

——. *Les Jouets à la World's Fair en 1904 à Saint Louis.* Paris: 1908.

——. *La Très véridique histoire de Nette et Tintin visitant le village du Jouet.* Paris: 1927.

AMACHER, RICHARD E. *Franklin's Wit and Folly.* New Brunswick, N. J.: Rutgers Univ. Press, 1953.

ANCELET - HUSTACHE, JEANNE. *Saint Nicholas.* New York: Macmillan, 1962.

AYRTON, M. CHAPLIN. *Child-Life in Japan and Japanese Child-Stories.* London: Griffith & Farran, 1879.

BARING-GOULD, S. *Strange Survivals.* London: Methuen, 1892.

BEARD, LINA, and ADELIA B. *Mother Nature's Toy-Shop.* New York: Scribner, 1918.

BEAUMONT, CYRIL W. *Flash-Back, Story of My Youth.* London: Beaumont, 1931.

BELLEW, FRANK. *The Art of Amusing.* London: Hotten, n.d.

BOEHN, M. VON. *Dolls and Puppets,* Revised Edition. Boston: Branford, 1956.

BOOTH, H. *Playthings.* New York: Bureau of Educational Experiments, 1917.

BRIDENBAUGH, CARL. *The Colonial Craftsman.* New York: New York Univ. Press, 1950.

BRUBAKER, MIRIAM. *A Century of Progress of Toys.* Washington: 1944.

CAMPBELL, M. W. *Paper Toy Making.* London: Pitman, 1937.

CANNING-WRIGHT, H. W. *Peeps at the World's Dolls.* London: Black, 1923.

CATA, J. M. *International Trade in Toys.* Washington, D. C.: U.S. Bureau of Commerce, Trade Information Bulletin No. 445.

CHAMBERLAIN, BASIL HALL. *Things Japanese.* London: Kegan Paul, 1890.

CHESTERTON, GILBERT KEITH. *Fancies Vs. Fads.* New York: Dodd, Mead, 1923.

——. *Tremendous Trifles.* New York: Dodd, Mead, 1909.

CHRISTENSEN, ERWIN O. *The Index to American Design.* New York: Macmillan, 1950.

CLARETIE, LEO. *Les Jouets, histoire, fabrication.* Paris: 1894.

——. *Une Collection des Poupees en Costumes Populaires.* Paris: 1901.

CLARKE, JOHN E. T. *Musical Boxes.* London: Allen & Unwin, 1961.

COLE, ADELINE P. *Notes on the Collection of Dolls and Figurines at the Wenham Museum.* Wenham Historical Association, 1951.

COLTON, HAROLD S. *Hopi Kachina Dolls.* Albuquerque: Univ. of New Mexico, 1949.

DAIKEN, LESLIE H. *Children's Games Throughout the Year.* London: Batsford, 1949.

——. *Children's Toys Throughout the Ages.* New York: Praeger, 1953.

——. *Teaching Through Play.* New York: Pitman, 1953.

Doll Collectors' Manual, 1949. The Doll Collectors of America, Inc., 1950.

Dolls. The Doll Collectors of America, Inc., 1946.

DOUGLASS, WINSOME. *Toys For Your Delight*. New York: Crowell, 1957.

DOW, GEORGE F. *Everyday Life in the Massachusetts Bay Colony*. Boston: Society for the Preservation of New England Antiquities, 1935.

————. *The Arts and Crafts in New England, 1704-1775*. Topsfield, Mass.: Wayside Press, 1927.

DOWDALL, HARRY G., and GLEASON, JOSEPH H. *Sham Battle*. New York: Knopf, 1929.

EARLE, ALICE MORSE. *Child Life in Colonial Days*. New York: Macmillan, 1899.

————. *Customs and Fashions in Old New England*. New York: Scribner, 1893.

————. *Diary of Anna Green Winslow*. Boston: Houghton Mifflin, 1894.

————. *Home Life in Colonial Days*. New York: Grosset & Dunlap, 1898.

————. *The Sabbath in Puritan New England*. New York: Scribner, 1891.

EARLY, ALICE K. *English Dolls, Effigies and Puppets*. London: Batsford, 1955.

EATON, ALLEN H. *Handicrafts of New England*. New York: Harper, 1949.

————. *Handicrafts of the Southern Highlands*. New York: Harper, 1937.

EATRIGHT, J. F., and YOUNG, B. M. *Adventuring with Toy Activities*. New York: Bureau of Public Teaching Colleges, Columbia University, n.d.

EDWARDS, AMELIA B. *Untrodden Peaks and Unfrequented Valleys*. London: Longmans, Green, 1873.

ELDRIDGE, CHARLOTTE. *The Godey Lady Doll*. New York: Hastings, 1953.

FAWCETT, CLARA EVELYN (HALLARD). *Dolls, A Guide for Collectors*. New York: Lindquist, 1947.

FOLMSBEE, BEULAH. *A Lay History of the Horn-Book*. Boston: The Horn Book, 1942.

FREEMAN, RUTH. *American Dolls*. New York: Century, 1952.

FREEMAN, RUTH and LARRY. *Cavalcade of Toys*. New York: Century, 1942.

GORDON, LESLEY. *A Pageant of Dolls*. New York: Wynn, 1949.

————. *Peepshow into Paradise*. London: Harrop, 1953.

GRANT, J. *The Doll's House*. London: Studio, 1934.

GRAVES, SARAH. *Bridge, the Short-tailed Whale*. Boston: Luce, 1949.

GROBER, KARL. *Children's Toys of Bygone Days*. London: Batsford, 1928.

HADDON, ALFRED C. *The Study of Man*. New York: Putnam, 1898.

HALE, CHRISTINA. *English Sports and Pastimes*. London: Batsford, 1949.

HEATHERINGTON, M. G. and UNDERHILL, M. C. *Simple Toy Making for Pleasure and Profit*. London: Pearson, 1925.

HERICK, EMANUEL. *Folktoys*. Prague: Artia, n.d.

HERTZ, LOUIS H. *Mechanical Toy Banks*. Wethersfield, Conn.: Mark Haber, 1947.

————. *Messrs. Ives of Bridgeport*. Wethersfield, Conn.: Mark Haber, 1950.

————. *Riding the Tinplate Rails*. Wethersfield, Conn.: Mark Haber, 1944.

————. *The Handbook of Old American Toys*. Wethersfield, Conn.: Mark Haber, 1947.

HINDLEY, CHARLES. *A History of the Cries of London*. London: Hindley, n.d.

HOKE, HELEN, and PELS, WALTER. *The First Book of Toys*. New York: Franklin, Watts, 1957.

HOLLIDAY, ROGERT C. *In the Neighborhood of Murray Hill*. New York: Doran, 1923.

HOLME, C. G. *Children's Toys of Yesterday*. Special winger supplement of *The Studio*, 1932.

HOOPER, ELIZABETH. *American Historical Dolls*. Baltimore, Md.: Privately published, 1952.

————. *Dolls the World Over*. Baltimore, Md.: Privately published, 1936.

HORTH, A. C. *I Made It Myself*. London: Batsford, 1941.

HOWARD, MARIAN B. *Homes for Paper Dolls and Kindred Paper Toys*. Miami, Florida: Franklin, 1953.

HUNT, W. BEN. *Kachina Dolls*. Milwaukee: Milwaukee Publishing Museum Popular Science Handbook, Series #7, Sept., 1957.

HUTCHINGS, MARGARET. *Glove Toys*. New York: Studio, 1958.

JACKSON, E. NEVILL. *Toys of Other Days*. London: Country Life, 1907.

JACOBS, FLORA GILL. *A History of Dolls' Houses*. New York: Scribner, 1953.

JOHL, J. P. *The Fascinating Story of Dolls.* New York: Lindquist, 1941.

———. *More About Dolls.* New York: Lindquist, 1941.

———. *Your Dolls and Mine.* New York: Lindquist, 1952.

JORDAN, NINA R. *The Home Toy Shop.* New York: Harcourt, 1937.

KAWIN, ETHEL. *The Wise Choice of Toys.* Chicago: Univ. of Chicago Press, 1934.

LAMBERT, M. and E. *English Popular Art.* London: Batsford, 1961.

LARWOOD, JACOB, and HOTTEN, JOHN C. *The History of Signboards.* London: Hotten, n.d.

LITTLE, NINA FLETCHER. *The Abby Aldrich Rockefeller Folk Art Collection.* Boston: Little, Brown, 1957.

LOW, FRANCES H. *Queen Victoria's Dolls.* London: Newnes, 1894.

MCCLINTOCK, INEZ and MARSHALL. *Toys in America.* Washington, D.C.: Public Affairs Press, 1961.

MCLEISH, M., and HORTON, WINIFRED M. *Wooden Toy Making.* Peoria, Ill.: Manual Arts Press, 1936.

Macy's Book of Sports and Pastimes. New York: Macy, 1885.

MAKINSON, J. T. *Toy Manufacturing.* New York: Funk & Wagnalls, 1931.

MEYER, JOHN D. *A Handbook of Old Mechanical Penny Banks.* Tyrone, Pa.: John D. Meyer, 1948.

MOCHRIE, E., and ROSEAMON, I. P. *Felt Toys.* Leicester, England: Dryad, 1949.

MOORE, COLLEEN. *Colleen Moore's Doll House; The Story of the Most Exquisite Toy in the World.* Garden City: Garden City Pub. Co., 1935.

MORLEY, HENRY. *Memoirs of Bartholomew Fair.* London: Routledge, 1892.

MUNTHE, AXEL. *Memories and Vagaries.* New York: Dutton, 1930.

OPIE, IONA and PETER. *The Lore and Language of School Children.* Oxford: Clarendon, 1959.

PEARCE, CYRIL. *Toys and Models.* London: Batsford, 1948.

ROSENBACH, A. S. W. *Early American Children's Books.* Portland, Maine: Southworth, 1933.

SHEPARD, ODELL. *The Joys of Forgetting.* Boston: Houghton, Mifflin, 1929.

SINCLAIR, H. *Toy Manufacturing and Marketing.* Springfield: Philips, 1931.

SINGLETON, E. *Dolls.* New York: Payson & Clarke, 1927.

STGEORGE, ELEANOR. *Dolls of Three Centuries.* New York: Scribner, 1951.

———. *Old Dolls.* New York: Barrows, 1950.

———. *The Dolls of Yesterday.* New York: Scribner, 1948.

STOWE, WILBUR MACY. *Paper Dolls and Other Cut-Out Toys.* Newark, N. J.: Newark Museum, n.d.

TANGERMAN, E. J. *Whittling and Wood Carving.* New York: Dover, 1936.

TEKIHO, NIXIZAWA. *Japanese Folk Stories.* Board of Tourist Industries, Japanese Government Railways, 1939.

TIPPET, J. S. *Toys and Toy Makers.* New York: Harper, 1931.

TOWNE, MORGAN. *Treasures in Truck and Trash.* Garden City, N. J.: Doubleday, 1949.

Toy Manufacturers in the U. S. A. New York: Toy Manufacturing Association, 1935.

TUMATSU, IWADO, M. A. *Children's Days in Japan.* Board of Tourist Industries, Japanese Government Railways, 1936.

USHER, ABBOTT P. *A History of Mechanical Inventions.* Cambridge: Harvard Univ. Press, 1954.

VAN ALSTYNE, D. *Play Behaviour and Children's Play Materials.* Chicago: Univ. of Chicago Press, 1932.

VELLAN, MARY. *Nursery Toys.* New York: Studio, 1956.

WARING, GEORGE E., JR. *Tyrol and the Skirt of the Alps.* New York: Harper, 1880.

WEISS, HARRY B. *Something About Jumping Jacks and Jack-in-the-Box.* Trenton, N. J.: Privately printed, 1945.

WHITE, C. T., and KAY, J. *Toys, Their Design and Construction.* Peoria, Ill.: Bennett, 1944.

WHITE, GWEN. *A Book of Toys.* New York: Penguin, 1946.

WILSON, A. E. *Penny Plain, Twopence Coloured.* London: Macmillan, 1932.

WRIGHT, ANNA ROSE, and JONES, RICHARD. *Children of the Nineties.* New York: Grosset & Dunlap, 1936.

WRIGHT, RICHARDSON. *Grandfather Was Queer.* Philadelphia: Lippincott, 1939.

———. *Hawkers and Walkers in Early America.* Philadelphia: Lippincott, 1927.

A Selected List of Stories About Toys

By PRISCILLA SAWYER LORD

ANDERSEN, HANS CHRISTIAN. "The Constant Tin Soldier." *The Complete Andersen.* Translated by Gene Hersholt. New York: Heritage, 1942.

————. "The Money-pig." *The Complete Andersen.* Translated by Gene Hersholt. New York: Heritage, 1942.

BAILEY, CAROLYN SHERWIN. *Miss Hickory.* New York: Viking, 1946.

————. "The Gingerbread Boy." *The Story Telling Hour.* ed. C. S. Bailey. New York: Dodd, Mead, 1934.

————. "The Rag Doll's Christmas." *A Book of Christmas Stories.* ed. Maude Walters Owens. New York: Dodd, Mead, 1931.

————. "The Soldier Who Lived in the Drum." *Stories for Sunday Telling.* Boston: Pilgrim, 1916.

————. "The Tinkling, Singing Music Box. *Ibid.*

————. *Tops and Whistles.* New York: Viking, 1937.

BAKER, MARGARET. *Victoria Josephine.* New York: Dodd, Mead, 1926.

BARNETZ, ELIZABETH DOWNING. *Bippy.* New York: Nelson, 1940.

BARRINGER, MARIE. *Martin the Goose Boy.* Garden City: Doubleday, 1932.

BEARD, EMMA PATTEN. *The Pantalette Doll from the Metropolitan Museum.* Chicago: Whitman, 1931.

BENSON, EDWARD FREDERICK. *David Blaize and the Blue Door.* New York: Doubleday, n.d.

BEST, MRS. ALLENA (CHAMPLIN). *Mon du Jos, the Story of a Little Black Doll.* Garden City: Doubleday, 1931.

————. *Strings to Adventure.* New York: Lothrop, 1935.

BIANCO, MRS. MARGERY (WILLIAMS). *Poor Cecco.* New York: Doran, 1925.

————. *The Adventures of Andy.* New York: Doran, 1927.

————. *The Little Wooden Doll.* New York: Macmillan, 1932.

————. *The Skin Horse.* New York: Doran, 1927.

————. *The Velveteen Rabbit; or How Toys Became Real.* Garden City: Doran, 1932.

BIANCO, PAMELA. *The Look-Inside Easter Egg.* New York: Oxford Univ. Press, 1952.

BLOCH, MARIE HAHN. *The Doll House Story.* New York: Walck, 1961.

BOWEN, WILLIAM ALVIN. *The Old Tobacco Shop.* New York: Macmillan, 1921.

BOYD, PEARL M. *Mike.* New York: Holt, 1928.

BRADBURY, BIANCA. *The Antique Gate.* Philadelphia: Carston, 1945.

BROCK, EMMA LILLIAN. *Drusilla.* New York: Macmillan, 1937.

————. *Little Fat Gretchen.* New York: Knopf, 1934.

BROMHALL, WINIFRED. "The Music Box." *Santa's Footprints and Other Stories.* New York: Aladdin Books, 1949.

BROWN, ABBIE FARWELL. "Balloon Boy." *Star Jewels and Other Wonders.* Boston: Houghton, Mifflin, 1905.

————. *The Lonesomest Doll.* Boston: Houghton, 1929.

BROWN, BEATRICE BRADSHAW. *A Doll's Day*. Boston: Little, Brown, 1931.

BURNETT, FRANCES HODGSON. *Racketty-Packetty House*. New York: Dodd, Mead, 1961.

CAUMERY. *Bécassine à Clocher-les-Bécasses*. Paris: Gautier-Languereau, 1958.

————. *Les Bonnes Idées de Bécassine*. Paris: Gautier-Languereau, 1958.

CAVANAH, FRANCES. *Jenny Lind and Her Listening Gate*. New York: Vanguard, 1961.

CHAPPELL, WARREN. *The Nutcracker*. New York, Knopf, 1958.

COATSWORTH, ELIZABETH. *The Children Come Running*. New York: Golden, 1960.

DALGLIESH, ALICE. *Little Wooden Farmer*. New York: Macmillan, 1930.

DeHUFF, ELIZABETH WILLIS. *Five Little Katchinas*. Boston: Houghton, 1930.

DIAZ, MRS. ABBY MORTON. *Polly Cologne*. Boston: Lothrop, 1930.

DOLBIER, MAURICE. *Torten's Christmas Secret*. Boston: Little, Brown, 1951.

DUMAS, ALEXANDRE. *The Nutcracker of Nuremberg*. New York: McBride, 1930.

ENCKING, LOUISE F. *The Toy Maker; How a Tree Became a Toy Village*. From the original of Gerda Thelen; retold by Louise V. Encking. Chicago: Whitman, 1935.

EWING, MRS. JULIANA HORATIA (GATTY). "The Land of Lost Toys." *Brownies and Other Tales*. London: Bell, 1924.

FARJEON, ELEANOR. *The Perfect Zoo*. Philadelphia: McKay, 1939.

FAULKNER, GEORGENE. *A Book of Christmas Stories for Children*. ed. Maude Owens Walters. New York: Dodd, Mead, 1930.

FIELD, RACHEL LYNAM. "Christmas in London." *Christmas* by Alice Dalgliesh. New York: Scribner, 1934.

————. *Hitty, Her First Hundred Years*. New York: Macmillan, 1929.

————. *Little Dog Toby*. New York: Macmillan, 1933.

————. *The Bird Began to Sing*. New York: Morrow, 1932.

FORBES, KATHERINE RUSSELL. *Dilly, A China Cat*. Boston: Lothrop, 1931.

FRANCHI, ANNA. *The Little Lead Soldier*. Philadelphia: Penn, 1919.

FREEMAN, MRS. MARY ELEANOR (WILKINS). "Jimmy Scarecrow's Christmas." *The Children's Book of Christmas Stories*. ed. Asa Don Dickinson and Ada Maria Skinner. New York: Doubleday, 1926.

GARNER, ELVIRA. *Sarah Faith Anderson: Her Book*. New York: Messner, 1939.

GODDEN, RUMER. *Candy Floss*. New York: Viking, 1959.

————. *Impunity Jane, the Story of a Bouquet Doll*. New York: Viking, 1954.

————. *Miss Happiness and Miss Flower*. New York: Viking, 1961.

————. *The Story of Holly and Ivy*. New York: Viking, 1957.

GOETZ, DELIA. *Pancheta, a Little Girl of Guatemala*. New York: Harcourt, 1941.

GRIMM. "The Golden Bird." *Household Stories*. New York: Macmillan, 1954.

GUTH, ZDENEK. Illustrator. *Little Christmas; or, How the Toys Come, a Story of a Little Boy, Far Away, Long Ago, and To-day*. New York: Macmillan, 1929.

HILL, HELEN, and MAXWELL, VIOLET. *Rudi of the Toll Gate*. New York: Macmillan, 1932.

————. "Toys and Christmas." *Christmas*, ed. Alice Dalgliesh. New York: Scribner, 1934.

HOLBERG, RUTH and RICHARD. *Mitty and Mr. Syrup*. Garden City: Doubleday, 1935.

HOUSMAN, LAURENCE. "Rocking Horse Land." *Moonshine and Clover*. New York: Harcourt, 1923.

HOWELLS, WILLIAM DEAN. *Boys Town*. New York: Harper, 1890.

HUGO, VICTOR. "Little Cosette." *For the Children's Hour*, ed. Carolyn Sherwin Bailey and Clara M. Lewis. Springfield, Mass.: Milton Bradley, 1906.

HUTCHINSON, VERONICA SOMERVILLE. "The Doll in the Grass." *Candlelight Stories*, ed. Veronica Somerville Hutchinson. New York: Minton, 1928.

JEWETT, SARAH ORNE. "The Water Dolly." *Play Days*. Boston: Houghton Mifflin, 1906.

JOSEPH, MRS. HELEN (HAIMAN). *Little Mr. Clown: The Adventures of a Marionette*. New York: Harcourt, 1932.

KNIGHT, MARJORIE. *Alexander's Birthday*. New York: Dutton, 1940.

———. *Alexander's Christmas*. New York: Dutton, 1938.

———. *Alexander's Vacation*. New York: Dutton, 1943.

LEIGHTON, CLARE VERONICAHOPE. *The Musical Box*. New York: Longmans, 1932.

LINDSAY, MAUD MCKNIGHT. *The Toy Shop*. Boston: Lothrop, 1926.

LORENZINI, CARLO. *Pinocchio in Africa* (translated from the Italian of Cherubini by Angelo Patri). Boston: Ginn, 1911.

———. *The Adventures of Pinocchio*. New York: Macmillan, 1935.

MILNE, ALAN ALEXANDER. *Winnie-the-Pooh*. New York: Dutton, 1926.

MOESCHLIN, ELSA. *The Red Horse*. New York: Coward-McCann, n.d.

MOORE, CLEMENT CLARK. *The Night Before Christmas*. New York: Crown, 1944.

MOORE, COLLEEN. *The Enchanted Castle*. Garden City: Garden City, 1935.

MORLEY, MARGARET WARNER. *Donkey John of the Toy Village*. Chicago: McClurg, 1935.

MORROW, MRS. ELIZABETH REEVE (CUTTER). *The Painted Pig*. New York: Knopf, 1930.

OTTO, MARGARET G. *The Tiny Man*. New York: Holt, 1955.

PARRISH, ANNE. *Floating Island*. New York: Harper, 1930.

PETERSHAM, MAUD and MISKA. *Get-away and Hary Janos*. New York: Viking, 1933.

PHILLIPS, ETHEL CALVERT. *Little Rag Doll*. Boston: Houghton, Mifflin, 1930.

POTTER, BEATRIX. *Tale of Two Bad Mice*. New York: Warne, 1904.

PYLE, KATHERINE. *The Christmas Angel*. Boston: Little, Brown, 1900.

RICHARDS, MRS. LAURA ELIZABETH (HOWE). "The Ambitious Rocking-Horse." *Joyous Story of Toto*. Boston: Little, Brown, 1913.

SANDBURG, CARL. "The Wedding Procession of the Rag Doll, and The Broom Handle," and "Who Was in It." *Rootabaga Stories*. New York: Harcourt, 1922.

SAWYER, RUTH. *The Little Red Horse*. New York: Viking, 1950.

SMITH, GERTRUDE. "A Merry Christmas." *A Book of Christmas Stories for Children* by Maude Owens Walters. New York: Dodd, Mead, 1931.

STEPHENSON, MRS. DELIA (MORRIS), and NELSON, RHODA. *Susan and Arabella, Pioneers*, by Rhoda Morris. Boston: Little, Brown, 1935.

STGEORGE, ELEANOR. *Old Dolls*. New York: Barrows, 1950.

THOMPSON, BLANCHE JENNINGS. *Silver Pennies*. New York: Macmillan, 1952.

TUDOR, TASHA. *The Dolls' Christmas*. New York: Oxford, 1950.

WIGGIN, KATE DOUGLAS, and SMITH, NORA ARCHIBALD. ed. "The Doll in the Grass." *Fairy Ring*. New York: Doubleday, 1934.

WILKINSON, WALTER. *The Peep Show*. New York: Stokes, 1932.

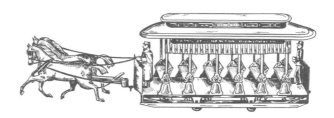

Index

DANIEL J. FOLEY

is a widely known horticulturist, author, and lecturer. From 1951 to 1957, Mr. Foley served as Editor of *Horticulture,* America's oldest garden magazine. A frequent contributor to newspapers and periodicals, a participant in radio and television programs, he holds membership in more than twenty specialized plant societies and professional organizations. In recent years he has traveled more than 50,000 miles visiting gardens and nurseries here and abroad.

Mr. Foley's interest in toys grew out of his earlier books, *Little Saints of Christmas, The Christmas Tree,* and *Christmas in the Good Old Days.*